To the Woods

To the Woods

Sinking Roots, Living Lightly, and Finding True Home

Evelyn Searle Hess

Oregon State University Press
Corvallis

The paper in this book meets the guidelines for permanence and durability of the Committee on Production Guidelines for Book Longevity of the Council on Library Resources and the minimum requirements of the American National Standard for Permanence of Paper for Printed Library Materials Z39.48-1984.

Library of Congress Cataloging-in-Publication Data
Hess, Evelyn Searle.
  To the woods : sinking roots, living lightly, and finding true home / Evelyn Searle Hess.
    p. cm.
  ISBN 978-0-87071-581-5 (alk. paper)
  1. Hess, Evelyn Searle--Homes and haunts--Oregon--Oregon Coast Range. 2. Oregon Coast Range (Or.)--Biography. 3. Country life--Oregon--Oregon Coast Range. 4. Nature--Effect of human beings on--Oregon--Oregon Coast Range. 5. Seasons--Oregon--Oregon Coast Range. I. Title.
  CT275.H5873A3 2010
  979.5--dc22
                                        2009054358

Oregon State University Press
121 The Valley Library
Corvallis OR 97331-4501
541-737-3166 • fax 541-737-3170
http://oregonstate.edu/dept/press

for Hannah

The Peace of Wild Things

When despair for the world grows in me
and I wake in the night at the least sound
in fear of what my life and my children's lives may be,
I go and lie down where the wood drake
nests in his beauty on the water, and the great heron feeds.
I come into the peace of wild things
who do not tax their lives with forethought
of grief. I come into the presence of still water.
And I feel above me the day-blind stars
waiting with their light. For a time
I rest in the grace of the world, and am free.

—Wendell Berry

Enough is as good as a feast.
—John Heywood 1497-1580, *Proverbs* pt 1

Contents

Preface

In our mid-fifties, my husband David and I left the toys and noise of urban society for the company of jumping mice, winter wrens, and dark nights full of stars and cricket song. Our twenty-one wooded acres in the Coast Range foothills had neither suffered nor benefited by civilization— meaning there would be no house, no electricity, no indoor plumbing in our new habitat, but it would be an exciting spot to develop our fledgling plant nursery.

To the Woods is the story of the land and fifteen years trying to uncover the secrets of its inhabitants while we learned to grow plants and to live very simply. That simple living connected us to the lives of the rest of the world's populace, most of whom live more simply still. Living close to nature revealed both the intricate interrelationships within ecosystems and their potential for fragility. I frequently found myself dancing between delight in the miraculous biosphere in which I played a minuscule part, and despair over the assault we hominids were perpetrating on it. At the same time, freedom from society's constant barrage of corporate brainwash gave me space to see myself less in terms of an ideal and more as a mere being, trying (and frequently failing) to do my best. But underlying those times of discovery, concern, revelations and mishap remained a nearly constant bubbling joy.

The book is divided into five parts. Part One describes the property and our activities there while we still lived in town, between 1986, when we bought the land, and 1992. Parts Two through Five are arranged by season, spring through winter, recording the natural history of the season as well as our activities from the time we moved to the woods until 2007, when I penned the last pages. With the exception of Part Two: Spring, which begins at the equinox but follows certain events through a three-year period, each section records events and musings occurring in the specified season from any of the fifteen years 1992 to 2007. Although chronological within a chapter, time can move back and forth through those fifteen years as we travel through the chapters and through the seasons.

Dear Reader, please don your week-in-the-mountains attitude, that wonderful state of mind that discards any need for watch or calendar: we eat when we're hungry, sleep when we're tired, go home when we must. The book orients to date when it matters, but flowers bloom, birds fly, rain falls according to the season, not the year. You are invited to relax and come along. Listen to the wind in the trees and the yipping of the coyotes and marvel with us at the miracle of this intricate web in which we're all enmeshed. Perhaps together we can decide how to save it for our children or at least to help them appreciate it while it's here.

Acknowledgments

Though I'd never been much of a gymnast before, I stood on many strong shoulders to find the completion of this book. I am indebted to Hannah Wilson, who encouraged me to commit my life-changing adventure to paper. And to both Hannah and Jake for reminding me I'm not riding this spaceship solo.

Immeasurable appreciation to John Daniel, who helped me find the right path to explore my journey and to Cecelia Hagen, who held my hand through the entire trip. John and Cecelia were the *sine qua non*, providing support to keep me moving forward, and guidance to help me clarify and deepen way stations along the route.

Thank you to Quinton Hallett and Charles Goodrich for careful reading and helpful suggestions. Thank you also to members of John's workshop, Cecelia's memoir class, and to Barbara, Patty, and Quinton from my Kwinnim writing group.

Scott Slovic took time from his life as professor and world lecturer not only to read the manuscript, but then to play agent and introduce me to Mary Braun, Acquisitions Editor of Oregon State University Press. Huge thanks, Scott. And thanks to Mary for two years of correspondence, and for engineering the necessary networks for the book's publication. To Micki Reaman and the marketing crew, great appreciation for your hard work, and thanks to Jo Alexander for careful reading, leaving the manuscript in better shape than she received it. Thanks also to all the OSU Press behind-the-scenes folks, unknown to me but no less valued.

I am grateful to Erika, Andrea, and Kim, all of whom I exploited shamelessly in the nursery's early years. Thank you to David for putting up with me, to Dr. Miller for returning him to me, and to Dorothy for making that possible. Thanks to Erika, Jeff, Nate, Celina, Tasha, and Camila for being such extraordinary people. It's a pleasure and honor to know you. And thanks to Bob, Rachel, Rebecca, Stephanie, and Danny for joining our family and enriching our lives.

I'm ever reminded of the boundless debt I owe to my original ancestors, the stars, the sun and moon, the atmosphere, the oceans, the microorganisms. Thanks also to my aunts, uncles, and cousins, the rocks and trees, the bryophytes, the flowering plants and invertebrates, and to my multitude of siblings, the running, creeping, flying, swimming vertebrates. We're all in this together, gang.

Thanks to *From Sawdust and Cider to Wine: A History of Lorane, Oregon and the Siuslaw Valley*, by Patricia Ann Edwards, from which I got much of the area history, and to Wendell Berry for his wonderful poem, "The Peace of Wild Things." He tells my story in just eleven lines. I am grateful also to John Heywood for a proverb known in the sixteenth century that so many in the twenty-first have yet to learn.

The events recorded in *To the Woods* are as accurate as memory allows. The people too are real, although a few names have been changed to preserve their privacy.

PART ONE

The Setting

Chapter One

I stumble groggily to the propane heater, match box in hand, twist open the tank valve, and depress the red button to the count of thirty. I scrape a match across the box and poke its flame into the small hole leading to the gas jet. Phoom! Push up the lever to adjust the roar and carefully carry the burning stick five paces to light the gas for the lantern and the Coleman stove. I shove the tea kettle onto the burner and blow out the remaining flame before it reaches my finger. Yay! I made it. All three on one match!

Generally David has the chill off the house before I'm up, but today he's in town for a breakfast meeting, giving me the opportunity to test my match-saving prowess. I squeeze out yesterday's green-tea bag, rubbing its soothing coolness on my bleary eyes before popping a fresh bag into my cup. Often I linger over the newspaper with my morning cup of tea but this morning I'm in a hurry. I want to settle into a favorite spot in the woods while the sun is still low in the eastern sky.

I sit halfway up the steep northeast slope of our woods, where Douglas firs with moss-draped limbs tower above me. Directly in front of me is a three-foot-diameter tree—perhaps a hundred years old—with a double top. Stubbed off long ago by lightning, maybe. I suppose that double top is what spared it from the chainsaw. Oceanspray and filbert make a lacey layer beneath the firs, and under that, scattered snowberry, herbaceous plants and moss. Even this deep in the woods the morning sun spins the moss to gold on the bottoms of dark-shrouded branches.

Thin, silvery silk lines shimmer between the trees, seeming suspended in space, their connections to the trees indiscernible. One spider's web looks like an old 45 record: an outer circle with threads so closely spaced it seems solid, and an open inner circle whose diameter is about the width of the outer band. Someone is home in the spindle-hole, but she's up too high for me to see well. Sunshine hits the top surfaces of deciduous leaves, turning on flat spots of light in the dark forest. Fir trunks appear extra dark in contrast to the sun-gold needles, moss, and leaves around them. Nearby a winter wren trills his long tinkling song.

Recently a friend asked if I believe in heaven. Sitting here, I wonder how I could not. I'm there!

It's still hard to believe this woods is ours—or at least ours to be a part of as long as we're around. In 1986 my husband, David, and I bought the land to accomodate a plant nursery, which was to be our retirement project. David had an active architecture practice and I was at the university, running the biology research and teaching greenhouses and teaching an occasional class. But we were looking ahead, and clearly there wasn't space on our city lot for a nursery.

Twenty-one acres we found. Twenty-one wooded acres wrapping around the north, east, and south sides of a hill, giving us elevations from six hundred to nine hundred feet. With all these different exposures, I knew I would be able to grow any plant I might ever want to try. The north side is shady and cool, rising abruptly, and carpeted with sword ferns that grow through several kinds of moss. Douglas fir trunks, fuzzy with moss and painted with splotches of silvery lichens, emerge from the fern cover, but to see their tops you have to tip your head till you crink your neck. Here and there at their feet are the decaying remains of their ancestors' stumps.

Between the sword ferns and the fifty-year-old firs are branches of filbert and osoberry, long known as Indian plum. These two are the trumpets to spring. They awaken in February when most of their companions are still asleep. The filbert's male flowers, rows of spun-honey exclamation points, become glowing chains with the sun behind them. If you look closely, you're rewarded with startling tiny, dark red, female flowers, gleaming like embers. Osoberry, the second player in the pre-spring fanfare, is the first forest shrub to leaf out. The new leaves perch along the stems like apple-green butterflies, wings held vertically over their backs. The equally early flowers are long clusters of pale yellow to greenish-white bells.

David's first change to the property was to reconfigure the driveway. At our initial visit, it shot straight up the middle of the northern meadow, continuing its unswerving path along the hill's east face until it turned abruptly at the south side of the hill, perching on a narrow terrace on the precipitous south slope. David immediately saw that if we entered instead at the base of the hill another fifty yards up the main road, the drive could follow the hill's form, providing a soft, welcoming entrance molded by the topography and leaving the meadow in one piece.

Walking the new driveway from the entrance off the main road, you have the steep north-facing slope to the right and a fairly level woodland to the left, mostly half-century-old firs mixed with filbert and a few Oregon white oaks. This flatter area opens to the meadow where we have sited our small nursery. The drive then curves to the base of the hill's east slope. Here the east and south sun warms the nursery, while the hill protects the plants from too much late afternoon heat.

As the drive begins to bend toward the south side of the hill, the flora changes. Oceanspray, red-flowering currant, blue elderberry, and grand fir join a quarter-acre patch of oaks as the land plunges sharply downward. Leathery lung-lichen falls from the oaks in the winter and garlands of silvery-gray lichen festoon the trees year-round.

From there you turn on to the south slope and—pow! You blast into a different country—bright and hot. The hillside was clear-cut a few years before we bought the property and replanted—much too densely—in Douglas firs intended to be Christmas trees, now thirty-foot-tall poles with feathery hats. The hill drops away to oaks, sarvisberry, cascara, and the ubiquitous Douglas fir that this property, like most of western Oregon, grows so well.

I'm sure I set my mouth and clamped my jaw when I wrote "sarvisberry." That's the name I always heard when I was growing up. In later years when I began reading "serviceberry" I felt defensive of the old familiar name and of my attachment to it. To me it implied that "sarvis" was a mispronunciation or corruption of "service." But my mother used words with care. She never used slang; she had impeccable grammar and diction. If she said *sarvisberry*, that's what it was. Or so I thought. But in fact, the name was what she in turn had grown up with, and therein lies the problem with common names.

The common names of plants change from place to place and from one decade to another. Some arouse your curiosity (Johnny-jump-up, Johnny-kiss-me-under-the-garden-gate,—kind of makes you wonder about Johnny, doesn't it?—love-in-the-mist, love-lies-bleeding, mourning widow—possibly it was her partner bleeding in the mist?) but tell little about the plant being named. Sometimes two different plants have the same common name and a single plant with several common names is not unusual. So I feel justified in sticking with sarvisberry, or if I want to ensure understanding—at least with folks speaking Botanese—the universally accepted *Amelanchier.*

Some writers proclaim naming itself to be a mistake. The argument, if I understand it, is that to name, and therefore to classify or categorize, claims ownership, and takes away from the essence of the item named, diminishing the mystery and wonder. I can't buy it. Would I love my children more, appreciate their uniqueness more, if they were child one and child two rather than Erika and Jeffrey? Or girl child and boy child? Or simply "human"? I will continue to learn the names of plants and animals and any other elements of this earth that I can cram into my brain. I feel more related to what I can call by name.

Back at the sunny hillside where sarvisberry grows along with cascara, oak, and Douglas fir, there are places where the driveway becomes little more than a narrow ledge cut into the slope. But at the full south exposure just above the drive, where we plan eventually to build our house, lies a terrace, the noon sun inviting us to operate on solar energy. Farther along and below the road, rough-skinned newts and water bugs swim in a year-round pond fed by the steep hills above.

It doesn't appear that anyone has ever built a house on this property. Philesta and David Boone Zumwalt arrived in Oregon from Illinois, in the fall of 1853. They filed for and received a 319-acre donation land claim, and the next year built a house and barn that are now on the Historic Registry and sit near the north edge of our hill, off Territorial Road. The Zumwalts had thirteen children but apparently built no other houses on the land. Louis Schaffer, a German immigrant, and his wife Louise came to Lorane around 1905. They bought six hundred acres east and south of us, and later added the Zumwalt place. Their son Charles logged most of the original Zumwalt claim, and then sold nearly three hundred acres to a developer, who subdivided it into approximately twenty-acre lots, one of which is our little piece of woods.

In the early twentieth century, hundreds of acres in the Lorane area and Siuslaw valley were planted to apple and pear orchards, primarily as a real estate venture. The largest orchard was about eighteen hundred acres, to be sold in small parcels to investors in Michigan and Wisconsin. The orchards are long gone but I like to think that the three old apple trees on our property are their progeny, probably planted by a bird or roaming bear.

I wonder sometimes if local tribes might have built one of their big plank and bark winter homes on this piece of the hill. I think it doubtful, though, because from what I read they tended to stay closer to the rivers, using higher land for hunting and camping rather than for building dwellings. This would have been a good spot for collecting acorns even if they didn't choose to build here.

On a colored map of the United States, most of the western portion is rendered in shades of brown—high deserts and mountains. A thin green fringe lies along the Pacific Coast, and narrow fingers of green reach into the interior valleys of Washington, Oregon, and California. Oregon has the reputation for being a soggy state, but in fact it rains very little outside of those small fringes and fingers, and not even there, to speak of, in the summer. Our property curves around a toe of one of the Coast Range foothills on the west edge of the southern end of the green Willamette Valley. A dead-end road rises through agricultural land until it turns at the corner of our property to parallel the spine of the hill with open land to the north and wooded properties to the south. Our land, like other properties on our side of the road, is long and narrow, the southern portion draping sharply over the south side of the slope.

Rights to a two-family water system came along with the property, helping our decision to buy the land for our nursery, and perhaps someday for a house site. Good wells are not easy to come by around here, with people reporting water containing arsenic or salt as well as simply low flow. Our hill has an underlying basaltic ridge that, in many places, makes access to the water table difficult or impossible. Our well was on a third lot farther up the hill, with pipes to the pumphouse on our neighbors' land, and from there to the borderline between their property and ours. We were glad this was legally sorted out before we bought our land, and relieved to have rights to a good well, even if we did have to share it.

The idea of sharing a well reminded me, with some anxiety, of the history of water wars between western farmers and ranchers when the area was being settled by the early pioneers. "Whiskey is for drinking," they used to say, "and water is for fighting." Water is an essential and precious resource, and disputes are understandable. Is the other guy using more than his or her share? Is he compromising the quality of *my* water?

Besides the fact of sharing the water, I am very aware of our droughty summers, and I don't want to waste a drop. I've been teased about that, in this land of abundant winter rain. When I was a child, if anyone left food on her plate, some adult was sure to scold, "Think of the starving Armenians!" I could never understand how eating all my food was going to help the Armenians. It seemed as if it would be more effective for us to eat less, and ship off the extra. But it isn't just the "Armenians" who will be affected by profligate use of water: local wells go dry as well. We try to remember that there is one worldwide supply of water through space and time—the same water that refreshed the dinosaurs waters my perennials—so David and I are committed to frugality.

We decided to dig a pond to irrigate our plants through water-efficient drip tubes. Fortunately, my nephew Jim was working on his master's degree in agricultural engineering and needed a project. He and a friend walked and surveyed the property and he found the perfect contours in a relatively level boomerang shape near the bottom of the south slope. He designed terraces above the road and determined how to direct the run-off from the hillside to fill the pond. The pond was to be eight feet deep, and approximately two hundred feet long. It would hold three and a half acre-feet of water.

So then we began the search for excavators. We got a number of estimates—and were totally devastated. Their figures were more than double our budget. But just when we were about to give up, we talked to a contractor whose estimate was close to what we had hoped. It was his uncle who had built our new entrance drive and we had liked both him and his work. The contractor's price was right, so based on that and liking his uncle, we hired him.

We were living in Eugene, some seventeen miles away, so we missed out on a lot of the work. But anytime we could schedule the commute around our jobs and other activities, we would come watch the backhoe digging, dump trucks hauling—for hours and days and weeks. I'm a bit of a fanatic about soil. With run-off from agriculture and logging, along with natural events, the world is losing soil at twice the rate it is being created. I certainly wasn't going to let the contractors bury or haul away any of the good topsoil they removed from the pond site, so I asked them to spread it where we would be building our display garden, and over the meadow. They used the remaining excavated material to level a large area below the pond, reaching to the property edge—an ideal location for a future greenhouse, I thought.

The hole for the pond got deeper and deeper, the high cut bank to the north disconcertingly steep. In landscape architecture classes I had learned the importance of honoring the "angle of repose"—the maximum slope taken by a cone of sand without losing grains down the side—to ensure stability of banks. This was clearly steeper than the angle of repose.

And then we discovered why the contractor's estimate had been affordable: it was his first pond, and he really didn't know what the job was going to entail. Before the project's half-way point, he had run through our budget. Our options were to pay him off and end up with a half-finished hole, or to find some more money. So we sold our remaining inherited stock certificates, and he kept digging.

It did give us pause: our entire savings had been wiped out for a huge dry hole. I have a picture of our then two-year-old grandson playing in a pile of dirt in the bottom of the hole, so I guess it had some benefit. But we trusted that winter would bring rain and the pond would fill, and we couldn't water the plants or quench animals' thirst with cash. I appreciated that money was the fuel powering the construction of the pond, but funds themselves had never been my security or my goal. My mother used to quote some lines by James Terry White: "If thou of fortune be bereft / and in thy store there be but left / two loaves—sell one, and with the dole / buy hyacinths to feed thy soul." My pockets were empty but I looked at that big dry hole and I could almost smell the hyacinths.

Our jobs in town left us little time for the nursery. Still, we tried to come out most weekends, hauling tools, fertilizer, and water. As soon as we could manage the time, we strung about three hundred feet of poly pipe down the hill from the boundary with our neighbor so we could access our mutual water supply. And we invested in a cheap used single-wide trailer to store supplies. At last we would waste less time loading and unloading, or worse yet, arriving to find we'd left something important at home.

Meanwhile, as days shortened and summer dwindled, the pond excavation presented an opportunity to learn a bit of local geomorphology. The soil substrate here is very old, dating from the middle Eocene (about fifty million years ago.) The soils are said to house fossil remains from when they were under the oceans (although I haven't found any) and include sandy or silty shales and mudstones. The contractor who dug the pond pulled a huge boulder from the hole and left it on the ground near a solitary Douglas fir. The boulder was about four feet in diameter and roughly spherical. On our various explorations of the land, we hadn't come across any rocks, so were pleased we actually had some. But we didn't have this one for long. Mudstone weathers into fine chips and flakes; and out in the air and the rain, our boulder disintegrated almost as we watched.

As it turned out, other such boulders were included in the fill that made the terrace where I had hoped to build a greenhouse. So it shouldn't have been a surprise to see the fill-terrace slump and slide and collapse, finally reaching an irregular grade a good four feet below where it started. Fortunately, even in our impetuous enthusiasm, we hadn't actually built the greenhouse yet.

But the rains that buckled the terrace filled the pond. What a thrill! Water ran down the hill, gurgled in the ditches, coursed through culverts and over more hillsides, where it ran into the pond, just as Jim had planned and we had dreamed.

Our pond would be just the beginning of great things to come. Such plans we had! Such excitement! We exemplified what David called, when contemplating a new building project, the "peeing all over the floor" stage.

Before the pond emptied our bank account we had bought a small Kubota tractor, so we could mow and till when necessary. But with all that new pond soil, it often wasn't necessary. The fall after digging the pond we bought scads of bulbs—narcissus, hyacinths, and more than three hundred tulips—which we planted at the entrance and in great drifts at the woods' edges. We brought in compost of chopped oak leaves and old sawdust, spread it over the topsoil from the pond, and planted twelve hundred blueberries of six varieties, to bear from early in the season nearly to fall. To the west of the blueberries we plotted beds to field-grow nursery plants, which would demand far less water than would plants in pots. We decided to emphasize Mediterranean plants for their drought tolerance, and planted beds of lavender, rosemary, and various sages. And we started working on the display garden. Inspired by the work of Britain's famous landscape designer Gertrude Jekyll, we decided to build a double border, each bed about ten feet deep and more than thirty feet long, which would make a rainbow of plants. It began with white flowers and gray and silver foliage to rest the eyes and prepare them for the sunset colors to follow. Then came reds, liberally laced with purple to keep the reds from fighting, proceeding to oranges and yellows. Next the colors cooled to blue (with a bit of white added to make the blues bluer), purple, and pink. We were very proud of our accomplishment.

Humus—the part of organic matter that is slowest to break down and that stores nutrients, as it aerates and holds moisture in the soil—is from the same word root as *humility*, and is as essential in the garden as humility is in the gardener, or in anyone else who tinkers with the ecosystem. It's such an illusion to think we can control anything in nature. I am regularly shown how powerless I am. I can't make it rain when my plants need a drink or keep it from raining when I need to weed. I can't dissuade the frosts from nipping new growth or the sun from sizzling it. And I definitely can't convince slugs, voles, and deer not to dine on something I consider precious.

As anyone who has lived in deer country knows, tulips are deer candy. Three hundred-plus tulips gobbled up in one quick lunch! Most of the rest of the bulbs added interesting flavors to the menu or were quickly dispatched by the squirrels and chipmunks. Narcissus—the daffodil clan—have bulbs that are toxic to many creatures so are considered deer-proof. Our deer agreed about the leaves, but found the flowers quite tasty. I wonder how many people grow daffodils just for the leaves.

I suppose I should have realized that front-end loaders, backhoes, and dump trucks are not exactly precision instruments when I asked to have the topsoil spread in the meadow and the subsoil used as fill beyond the pond, but I was completely unprepared for the results. The precious topsoil I considered so important to save from the pond excavation got lost in the excavated subsoil—a sticky clay—all of which buried the good native topsoil on the garden site. Along with the clay came yards and yards (perhaps miles and miles) of chopped Canada thistle root to which I was—for a while—completely oblivious.

A season or two after our big planting binge, thousands of Canada thistles came up where no thistle had been before, throughout the blueberries and the display bed. Ideally we'd have been patient and waited at least a season to plant, but in our fervor, we had had to do it *now*. Or, once we saw the invaders, if we'd been a little bit prudent, we'd have removed all of our fall plantings and gone after the thistle. But we weren't and we didn't.

More than a decade later we are still fighting thistles whose roots are under, around, and in whatever we try to grow. An ag inspector once told me that he had seen thistle rhizomes more than twenty feet long in roadway cut banks. Thistles bud vertically off a long underground rhizome and if you pull one up, you are just breaking it off, not getting rid of it. If you rototill an area with thistles present (which we have done) you chop the roots and rhizomes into little propagules. One becomes one hundred.

The moral to this sad story is, don't ever spread something on the soil if you don't know what it is! Intellectually, I knew that. I've heard countless horror stories covering hundreds of years to the present. I have read how a farmer in Kent, England, plowed into his fields straw bedding that had been used by injured soldiers returning from the Napoleonic wars. Mixed with the straw was thanet cress, a terribly invasive weed that then spread throughout England, where it remains firmly established.

And the story keeps getting re-told. In the early 2000s in the Pacific Northwest, an organic farmer spread manure-laced straw from his stables onto his fields, as had always been his practice, only to discover that the straw, which he had purchased, had been sprayed with triclopyr, a herbicide that is extremely slow to break down. What seemed to be safe and effective husbandry killed acres of tomato plants.

But herbicide isn't necessary to kill plants. Our next painful discovery was that although our long dry summers do put us in the "Mediterranean climate" category, a typically wet western-Oregon winter soaks up that clayey fill soil, and quickly rots the roots of Mediterranean plants. So we would have to grow in pots after all, and would try a wide variety of herbaceous plants—"everything you need for your perennial border."

We were frustrated by all of our ignorance and missteps, but undaunted. After years of gardening, I had thought I knew what I was doing, but I began to realize that gardening in town—in a human-controlled environment—was a far different thing from trying to impose my ideas on relatively undisturbed ground. And once I did disturb the ground, I'd better either think it out well or be prepared to take the consequences. As immigrants in a new land, we needed to learn the language and the customs, to pay attention, and to think before we acted.

Chapter Two

Two years after buying our property I left my job at the University of Oregon. It had been a stimulating and rewarding job that I thought I would keep until retirement—a minimum of six more years. But there were organizational changes, and priority and emphasis changes, and politics and personalities became a consideration. Never one to let practicality and security trump happiness and challenge, I decided ten years was enough.

Our daughter, Erika, had become uncomfortable in her job as well. She and I had received our masters' degrees the same year—hers in French literature from the University of Washington; mine an interdisciplinary degree in landscape architecture, horticulture, and journalism from the University of Oregon. She was twenty-nine; I was fifty-two. Her boyfriend had expended some effort putting up with her master's studies, and was less than enthusiastic about the prospect of her continuing. So when they returned to Eugene, she took a job with a media firm. But that quickly lost its luster, as her relationship was also beginning to do.

She suggested that, along with our fledgling nursery, she and I could start a garden service together. I never would have thought of that. I had run some wholesale greenhouses but had never done independent manual labor for pay—plus, I was in my early fifties. But it did seem like a way to leave the university and make a living while we were building the nursery.

We quickly got plenty of work. There were lots of mow-blow-and-go guys around, but few who really knew about plants, who wouldn't pull out the tulips and leave the bull thistle. Our first big job was to re-design and re-build the garden of friends of a friend. We started by removing a huge bed of ivy—about ten by forty feet. This was intense, dense, old-growth ivy with stumps more than three inches across, and tangled growth clambering over the fence and rooting in beds on the other side.

First we had to cut off the confusion of top growth and dig or pull the many places it had rooted along the stems. Then we grubbed out the main crown and roots. My favorite tool was—and still is for such jobs—a mattock, a heavy tool with an ax handle and a long flat hoeing blade on one side and a shorter chopping blade on the other. I am no Amazon.

13

I'm about five foot two and my muscles are okay for an old woman, but nothing to write home about. But a mattock is the great equalizer. It felt really good to be able to work, to push my animal body. At the end of the day I would be exhausted, but exhilarated that I was able to ask that much of my body and get a generally positive answer.

I became quite *macha*. I bristled when someone was solicitous of this middle-aged woman, offering to do the heavier jobs, and would think, *I don't care if you're younger and stronger, I can do it. Especially if you happen to be younger and stronger and male, I can do it.*

I always was a bit of a tomboy—or an animal girl might be a better description. I spent half of my young life up trees. A big willow towered near the house where I grew up, a couple of miles south of the little western Washington town of Chehalis. It had a high perch where I would spend hours through most of the 1940s looking out to the horizon, lost in my imaginings. I wish I could remember some of those reveries. But I just remember how completely at home I was there, gazing out.

My first major accident involved a tree. When I was nine years old, my big sister Nancy and I climbed high in a Douglas fir. I was fifty or so feet up and she maybe ten feet below me when a neighbor boy and his mother came to visit. We started climbing down but Nancy wasn't going fast enough to suit me so, impatient and impulsive, I scrambled around her. I'm not truly sure what happened next but I always told people that I grabbed a dead branch and stepped on one that wasn't there. The effect is right even if the facts aren't quite.

I still remember the surreal feel of plummeting through the branches, although to me it seemed more like a slow-motion float than a plummet. About ten feet above the ground, two branches that came out of the trunk in a "V" shape broke my fall for an instant. I remember thinking, *I'm finally down.* As soon as I got the thought out, I kept going, landing on an exposed root of the tree. I was briefly unconscious but awoke gasping and my breath came in sobs for hours. I was chagrined that the neighbor boy might think I was crying. I was no sissy!

I had a couple of broken ribs and another that was cracked, plus many bruises, but felt only my bruised pride until the next day. Our logger neighbor figured I'd fallen at least forty feet, and it was a miracle I was alive or hadn't at a minimum broken my neck or back. But little animal-girl bones are strong and resilient. I wouldn't want to try it now.

So the animal woman and her daughter kept battling the ivy. It seemed it would take forever, and the man of the house wondered why we didn't just get in there with a rototiller and make short work of it. That would have been a nice mess. Chopping ivy roots is an effective way to propagate it, plus those long, sinuous stems would wrap tightly around the tiller blades within minutes.

Eventually we won the battle. The owners hadn't budgeted, though, for the new fence they had to build. With the removal of the ivy, the fence came tumbling down. The ivy had helped decay the fence and was eventually the only thing holding it up.

It turned out to be a lovely garden—the first of many—and a perfect way to use the perennials we grew in our fledgling nursery. Erika was wonderful to work with: smart, organized, supportive, and superlative company. If I got discouraged, she bucked me up. If I got scattered, she helped sort things out. And she was a tremendously good sport about working in less than ideal weather. One of my stand-out memories is of a day we were working in the cold in a yard on a loop road, high on a hill. We were trying to prune a mugho pine, but our hands kept getting too numb to function. We'd swing our arms, flap our hands, stamp our feet, and try again. Finally, all bundled up in layers of sweaters and wearing stiff over-sized raingear and rubber boots, we would run a lap on the loop road and come back to prune some more.

We got to be experts at locating public restrooms. I've read complaints about workpeople being so discourteous as to ask to use their employer's facilities, and heard of people who were shocked to see a homeless person peeing on the street. I wonder if contractors, gardeners, the homeless—outdoor people—are supposed to have differently functioning anatomies.

Anyway, we learned which stores had available restrooms and in which we would need to request a key, which parks had facilities and which were likely to be closed. One time, in a moment of need, after checking sight lines to the windows of the house where we were working, I squatted discreetly, I thought, in the woods. Within minutes the lady of the house called out cheerfully, "Hello! How are you today? If you ever need a drink or to go to the bathroom, just knock on the door!" With considerable embarrassment I realized that her neighbor higher on the hill had probably spotted me and given her a call.

I got my first personal glimpse of discrimination by stereotyping one day when I was dashing single-mindedly toward a store's plumbing. I had just crawled out of someone's garden: muddy hands, muddy knees, a smudge on my face, and my tousled hair full of plant debris. As I rushed through the store a woman stopped me, glared at me from hair to shoes and back again, and read me out. I was a "slut" and a "whore" and how did I dare associate with respectable people like her? I was so stunned by her vitriol I was speechless. I may have smiled weakly and muttered something inane like, "And a nice day to you, too," but with a sick feeling in my stomach, I played it over in my mind all day. I thought of scintillating repartee like, "Well if you'd ever done a lick of work in your life ..." And wondered if she would have accepted soiled clothes and hands on a man, assuming them to be the product of honest work. But once I slowed down my offended inner monolog, it occurred to me that there are great groups of people for whom, because of the way they look or speak, be it their coloring, their accent, their apparent poverty, or some physical abnormality, rude treatment is not uncommon. It was a good lesson for me.

Erika and I did a bit of stereotyping ourselves. We played a game where we would try to guess people's politics by looking at their yard. Beautifully groomed emerald green lawns, carefully clipped shrubs, and immaculate bark-mulched beds belonged, we reasoned, to Republicans. Loose, even wild, naturalistic gardens, with perennial borders and leaves in the flower beds, we thought to be the domain of Democrats. The funny thing was we were rarely wrong.

After twenty-five years of practicing architecture, David was getting restless. Two years after Erika and I started the business, he joined us. He said he was in his "instant gratification period." We could make a garden far faster than he could design a building and get it built.

Then Erika went back to school as a predoctoral student in French literature. I was thrilled for her but at the same time I felt as if I had a huge rock in my stomach. I wasn't at all sure I could manage—physically or psychologically—without her. Erika was a natural scholar. She had been an avid reader since she was very young. Now she wrote well, was an outstanding teacher, and loved learning. My head was in complete support. My gut wasn't so sure. But I knew she had found her appropriate road. David and I were on our own.

In the summer of 1991, our son Jeff, a southern Oregon high-school English teacher and track coach, moved with his wife, their six-year-old son, and four-year-old daughter to Eugene for required graduate courses at the university. About a mile south of the university, our house was an easy walk or bike-ride away. We relished the chance to see more of them and hated to think of them having to put out rent money, so encouraged them to stay with us. But in time, the crowded house seemed to take a toll, especially on our daughter-in-law.

One day at the nursery David and I had a brainstorm. We had the old single-wide trailer we had hauled in to store fertilizer and tools. Why couldn't we push aside some of the equipment, put down a mattress, and spend the rest of the summer near our plants? We would commute to work instead of to the nursery, giving our visiting family some space and privacy. So we bought a two-burner Coleman stove, looked for a spot to dig a latrine, and prepared for a summer of camping.

We discovered the stars. Having been on our property only in daytime, we had not appreciated the benefits of seeing the night sky without competition from city lights. The stars, the moon, had never been brighter.

We stood outside the trailer door and gazed up to sky in the shape of a piece of pie with a big bite out of the tip. The tops of black-green Doug fir made a jagged border around the wedge; pink chiffon and cotton candy clouds were strewn across the darkening blue. Big brown bats zoomed this way and that, over our heads and over the tree tops, doing aerial gymnastics as they nabbed mosquitoes, moths, and termites. Crickets sang their evening chorus, which would become a steady pulsing trill by the time the stars covered the sky. About 2:30 one summer morning the Leonid showers left me gasping as I watched one flaming meteor after another paint arcing trails across the dark. I couldn't imagine how I could be so lucky as to live in the midst of all this.

Having more daytime hours on site was a gift as well. We had been thrilled when our pond had filled but we hadn't stopped worrying about it, and staying there gave us a chance to keep closer tabs. Well into the summer it still held water, so that was reassuring. But looking across the reflecting water to the steep and naked north bank, its cornices already under-cut, I had visions of erosion eventually washing out the road above. If the bank below it slid, the narrow road so close to the top of the bank would surely go with it. We began knocking off the cornices, smoothing out the top of the slope. In an attempt to stabilize the soil, we planted red-twig dogwood cuttings in horizontal bundles called fascines. The fascine itself helps reinforce the bank, as would a log, and then adds soil stability when cuttings root, and shoots spouting from leaf buds protect the soil surface. We watched a young oak growing on precipitous wet soil near the pond loosen its hold and fall into the water. It was followed by several other trees. An old oak stood high on the east bank, a third of its roots dangling bare. The soil behind it separated from the slope above and settled to a terrace as much as three feet below, but the tree continued to live and remain upright.

We were also alarmed to see a leak toward the top of the dike, along the south edge of the pond's boomerang shape. We wondered what the water pressure might do. Would the dam break and a million gallons of impounded water rush down the hillside to flood Territorial Highway below us? Might a wall of water hit a car? What might the damage be to the soil, to the plants and soil-dwelling animals? Fortunately there were no homes between the pond and the valley floor.

On a visit to a farm store we picked up bags of bentonite, a fine ash-based clay that seeks holes and is able to absorb great quantities of water, causing the clay to swell and act as a plug. Dumping the bentonite into the pond seemed to solve the worst of the problems but it didn't keep us from having nightmares about catastrophes. So far, however, they have been nightmares without cause. Over time just one small leak refused to be stopped. It is high on the dam and regularly lowers the water from its highest level, letting it trickle onto the cratered area below. The spot I originally saw as a greenhouse site has become a rich wetland.

I never stopped worrying about the pond, but mostly we just appreciated knowing it was there while we worked elsewhere. When we were commuting to the nursery, we had come with a goal: amending the soil, planting, weeding, fighting blackberries. But being there every day allowed us to focus more widely, to pay attention.

We began noticing numerous holes in our display garden, most of them about an inch and a half in diameter. There were none of the pushed-up earth hills or fans characteristic of moles and gophers—just holes. Then plants started dying or disappearing. Stems and leaves would come loose in my hands with no connection to crowns or roots. Whole plants would be pulled into the holes. It is a startling thing to watch a plant wiggle, wiggle, wiggle, and then sink out of sight.

Lois, our wildlife-biologist niece, identified this as the work of voles, fat little rodents also known as field mice. By the looks of things we must have had hundreds of voracious voles. We read everything we could find on controlling them but were not very happy with the results of our research. We refused to use poison. Trapping would be futile. And that pretty much covered the suggestions. Then a local farmer recommended carbon monoxide. We would hitch a hose to the exhaust pipe of the tractor and push the other end into a vole hole. The gas would travel from the tractor through the interconnecting tunnels, asphyxiating the voles. It seemed extreme, but gassing them wouldn't endanger their predators, and losing so many plants made us desperate.

So we covered dozens of holes with cardboard and newspapers, connected the hose and started the motor. I kept seeing little puffs of smoke coming from the ground—one here, one over there, one right beside me. Apparently we hadn't done the best job of covering the holes. After what seemed a very long time, but was probably only about ten minutes, I yelled to David that we had to stop. I didn't know about the voles, but *I* was feeling dizzy, and sick to my stomach from the fumes.

We may have decreased the population a bit, but we still had voles and I was still frustrated—not so much from losing the battle as from having fought the war. I began questioning the very idea of pests, of desirable wildlife and undesirable wildlife. What makes a creature a pest, anyway? The ones that annoy me are the ones that interfere with my agenda. But is my agenda more important than theirs? I suspect we annoyed the *voles* a bit with our carbon monoxide trick.

After a season or two, plant loss to voles declined to a minimal level. Perhaps it was worse initially because the loose soil of our new garden was an attractive and accommodating habitat for them, and it became less inviting as the soil settled. Or perhaps the explosion of voles lured enough predators, both wild and domesticated, that a rough balance was reached. I had personal experience with a small part of that balance. One Mothers' Day morning I went into the bedroom and discovered that the cat had brought me a present—a fat Mothers' Day vole—deposited daintily on my pillow.

But that was much later—well after our wonderful summer on the land. That summer came to an end. Jeff and his family moved back to southern Oregon for the new school year and we moved back to town and into our old hectic routines. When our daughter and son were around twelve and ten, they had a least chipmunk (*Tamias minimus*), who spent his days running around and around on the wheel in his cage. He would occasionally run upside-down across the top of the inside of the cage, especially when the cat lurked there and the chipmunk could teasingly run across the bottoms of the cat's feet. But mostly he just ran round and round and round on the wheel. In many ways it seemed our lives had become like that.

David and I were barely eighteen when we met, back in the mid-winter of 1954. We were University of Washington freshmen on a blind date arranged by David's friend Ted and Ted's girlfriend Phyllis, a friend of mine from the dorm.

A dormmate who ended up in Hollywood—I'll call her Martha—thought David was just about the most gorgeous hunk of male flesh she had ever set eyes on. Well-muscled from running track and milking cows, and with thick dark-blond curly hair, he looked to her (as she told me more than once) just like a Greek god. She would lean onto the reception desk and squirm seductively if she happened to be on duty when he came to call, checking him out with her big eyes half concealed under lowered lashes. Whatever raises a dog's hackles would soar within me, but David's response to her was so casual that the hackle-juices quickly subsided. Martha left school the next year, which didn't break my heart, and headed for Tinseltown. She was in a few films and eventually married Cary Grant, who didn't look a thing like David.

I wasn't personally acquainted with any Greek gods, but David's curly hair, gray-blue eyes, ruddy skin, and high cheekbones were definitely looks I wanted to know better. He had a quick smile and slightly prominent canines that, if he pulled his lips tight, he could push over the edge of his lower lip, Dracula-style, to illustrate a desired mood in a story. (He could also wiggle his ears, a talent he apparently used to amuse people behind him in classrooms.)

David introduced me to jazz. He had played trombone and drums in dance bands through junior high and high school, worrying his mother that he would become a junkie.

I introduced him to plant names, which I had learned from my botany-speaking mother. He loved the rhythm of their names, and I discovered that if I taught him one, he would retain it and could remind me when I forgot. He particularly enjoyed multi-syllabic and mellifluous sounds like *Liquidambar styraciflua, Metasequoia glyptostroboides,* and *Polygonatum odoratum variegatum.*

Our dates were mostly walks around campus and the university district. We spent much of our time looking up into the shadows and shapes of the leafy layers of a campus sycamore tree, or wandering the paths of the arboretum. Sometimes we would walk along Portage Bay, which connects Lake Washington to Lake Union, and admire the yachts and houseboats. I loved the water and as I talked dreamily about all the boats I'd like to have—canoes, sailboats, maybe a motorboat—he worried quietly about my acquisitiveness. We talked almost non-stop. He had a great memory for detail and could tell stories and remember facts and figures about a multitude of subjects, especially music and sports. We window-shopped along "the Ave" (the main drag in the university shopping district) and had long conversations with lonely old people who also were wandering and looking. David is more outgoing than I and easily struck up conversations with strangers, which we both found interesting and stimulating.

As we walked and looked, we compared dreams and plans for the future, never suggesting that it might be a shared future, but with an undercurrent of understanding that possibility. We became not only sweethearts but best friends. As I hung out with him in the architecture building, looking at his and his classmates' projects, I began to feel he was having more fun than I was. I was a journalism major and loved writing, but I felt less and less cut out for the pace and tension of the newspaper world. I was having a wonderful time in my field-botany class and it occurred to me that I could combine the plant world with the world of art and architecture. In the best of worlds, I would then write about what I learned.

Those were the days of the draft, so after our sophomore year David joined the army. The Korean War was over and the Vietnam War had not yet begun. David was stationed safely but boringly stateside. Buddies who joined with him were sent to Germany and Japan. I transferred to the University of Oregon to major in landscape architecture, as there was then no program at UW. I loved my major, found the UO and Eugene rather provincial compared to UW and Seattle, but pleasant, and deeply missed my friend. Many were the nights I would go for long walks, mixing tears with the rain.

At last, after his two years at Ft. Bliss in Texas and Ft. Stewart in Georgia, David joined me in Oregon. We were both excited to be opening a new chapter on our lives. There were some uncomfortable moments for him, joining me and my friends with none of his own, and some uneasiness with independent life after two years of being a good soldier (doing as he was told.) But he adjusted. He makes friends easily and we were happy to be together.

A year later, in September of 1958, we were married and I immediately got pregnant. I tried to finish my last year of school (my sixth, due to change of school and major), taking nineteen credit hours, working thirty hours a week, and trying with difficulty to pay attention to business rather than the life growing within me. David finished that year of school but, with a child on the way, he needed a job. A good draftsman, he got work first with steel fabricators, then with the county planning office, and eventually with an architectural firm. At first the jobs complicated school for him; then they took its place. I counted the minutes between labor pains as I sat in the library trying to study for spring term finals. I did take one exam after our beautiful daughter was born, but mostly got incompletes that year. Eighteen months later we were blessed with a boy baby, and I put my studies temporarily (I hoped) on hold.

I wonder how many people—especially very young people (we were three months shy of twenty-three when we married)—can hang on to their dreams while they struggle with too much work, too little sleep, worrying about new jobs, about pleasing the client, the boss, the partner, worrying about money, and focusing more on the children than on each other. In retrospect, I think it can be done with enough talking and listening. We talked about what was going on at work or with the children but were brought up in an era of not discussing feelings. Phrases like "Make the best of it," "Keep a stiff upper lip," "Smile and the world smiles with you," summed up the wisdom of the day. So we smiled and stayed busy—too busy. We escaped from our anxieties and disconnection in alcohol, in outside activities and friends. I have a memo on my refrigerator, "Action Absolves Anxiety." To an extent, that maxim is true. Action (work, projects, athletic training) fills time and can fulfill as well, but if it takes the place of real communion, it doesn't do much for a relationship.

I suppose it's at this point that many unions dissolve. If the handsome prince and his fairy princess find the sledding rougher than planned, the simplest thing might be to slide away in opposite directions. But we truly wanted to be together, so we tried to ignore the unnamed simmering frustrations. Together we supported our children in their activities. They grew and left for college. David continued to practice architecture; I worked at the university. We became active in plant groups and made plans to develop a nursery.

Now thirty-two years married, we worked side by side at our new joint venture, a nursery and garden service. We worked harmoniously with mutual caring and respect but I couldn't bring myself to be content with peaceful co-existence. I wanted exuberant emotional intimacy. Maybe I still believed in fairy tales.

After we moved back to our house in town, we spent our days landscaping other people's yards. Garden service was interesting but demanding, taking time from the nursery, which I wanted to be my focus. I was a poor businesswoman, caring more about the finished look of the garden in question than about the income it brought. And though our jobs were many, they were unpredictable, certainly never giving the guarantee of monthly salary I had known at the university.

We also needed to find a way to pay for medical insurance. I was able to continue in a university insurance group for eighteen months, but then we had to manage it on our own. A couple of years before I left the university, bacteria that cause ear infections in children took a wrong turn and ended up in my larynx. Barely able to breathe, I ended up under an oxygen tent in intensive care for a few days. Had that not happened, we probably wouldn't have bothered with the extra expense of insurance. But that experience caused caution to overcome frugality.

November property-tax time came and for the third consecutive year we realized we wouldn't be able to make the payment. I fought a building panic that we would get so far behind on taxes we'd lose the house. We had mortgaged the house to buy the property, so the loss of the house would mean losing the land as well.

Eventually the proverbial light bulb went on in my head. We had really enjoyed our summer on the land, living in the woods and being able to watch over the nursery. We could easily get renters in our house, close as it was to the university, and the rent would pay the mortgage as well as the overdue taxes. It was 1991, and it would be at least ten years until we could build the house we'd planned, but we had lived in the storage trailer for a summer, so we knew we could do it again. It's true it had neither plumbing nor electricity, but we would make do—and I had the unspoken hope that living together in the woods would dissolve that thin partition between us.

David agreed that it seemed not only a rational solution, but possibly a great adventure. It could be an answer for our financial difficulties; it was a tantalizing challenge; it would be a respite from the noise and the pace of town. We didn't guess what it would teach us about ourselves and our relationships, not only with each other, but with the whole world. Nor could we have imagined what the Fates had up their sleeves for our relatively near future.

So like thousands of pioneers before us, we charted our course west, searching for new lives, renewed hope, and the fulfillment of dreams.

Chapter Three

I felt pure excitement—no trepidation, no ambivalence—about our planned enterprise. But preparing for the move was something else again. We had been remodeling our house for fifteen years and now we had to get it finished and ready for renters. Besides that, we had thirty years of accumulated stuff to deal with. Most of it we gave away or threw away. Some (too much) we put in storage. As little as possible—but, we hoped, as much as necessary—would come with us.

Each thing needed to be evaluated and sorted, and the items were not mere things but memories, attachments, pieces of our lives. It was heartbreaking to find a precious memento destroyed by the moisture of the basement, but what hurt was not the loss of the item but the loss of what it stood for: memories of my parents, dead ten years; memories of my babies and little children, gone too, into adulthood. I helped them grow, encouraged their independence, and was proud of the adults they had become. But seeing little dresses and coats, dolls and toy swords, first- and second-grade drawings and stories, I was hit full face with the fact that these little people were no more, and would never return.

In the midst of our emotional turmoil and the physical exhaustion of sorting and hauling, plus David's and my growing irritability as we took the moving stresses out on each other, the boys who were to be our first tenants began pushing to get in. I felt as if I had a pack of wild dogs nipping at my heels. *Faster! Go faster!* And all the time, I wanted to linger over my memories. I was more than a little resentful. I wanted to scream or cry. I was ready to burst.

Eventually we decided the remodeling was good enough for now and what wasn't sorted could be pushed out of the tenants' way. In December of 1992 we packed up our dogs and cat and headed for our island of tranquility. After six years of commuting thirty-four miles from town to nursery and back, and about a year of working on the house, organizing, and packing, we were at last making the big move. The hills and the trees and the stars welcomed us home. We immediately relaxed, both physically and emotionally. We began our venture hand in hand, seeing these twenty-one acres as our true habitation, not the dilapidated storage trailer where we would cook and sleep.

The trailer is two and a half good paces across, and less than five times that long. Before we had it hauled out to the land to be our storage shed, it had been someone's modest home. Its narrow rectangle houses two rooms: a living room and a bedroom. In the wasp waist between those rooms are sink, stove, refrigerator, and closet-sized bathroom, all of which would have been useful if we had had electricity or plumbing. Our Coleman stove (*DANGER! Carbon monoxide hazard! Never use this appliance in an enclosed space*) sits on the built-in range. Because it is well insulated, the range's oven stays cool even in the hottest weather, making it a great place to store food. The refrigerator is too airtight to keep food in. I used to keep seeds in it until they began to mold from lack of air circulation. As I write this the fridge is plastered with aphorisms and pictures of our grandchildren and topped with book boxes, but the inside sits empty.

Across from the front door an eight-by-four-foot space called a tip-out makes a sort of bay window, and mitigates somewhat the narrow bus-like feeling of the space. Originally this was where we put David's drafting table, and I claimed the desk to the right of the door, at the end of the living room. About four feet from the desk we set up a card table, and to the left of the front door, a chest. These plus two chairs filled the living room.

One of the more elegant touches was our fancy "plumbing," which we came up with after a year or so of using a latrine—a big hole where we would throw fresh soil after use. Short pipes now go from the sink and toilet to outside buckets. We segregate our bathroom deposits—liquids only in the house toilet, solids in the outhouse up the road. The toilet is flushed with used dish-water and the bucket gets dumped on the compost pile. The outhouse is one of those portable pots the leasing company services regularly. The vacuum tank on the company truck sucks out the contents, excrement and fluid, and refills it with smelly blue liquid. We had it brought out when I hired some day laborers to help for a couple weeks, kept it when relatives came to visit, and keep it still. With memories of a portable sanitation company dumping its tank contents directly in the river, I called to be sure our company was emptying and treating the material responsibly. They explained that the pumper himself, as well as the disposal system, were DEQ certified. In processing, the tank contents are separated, with the liquid component pumped into the city sewer system. Once the solids are dry, organism numbers are diminished, as most of their food supply has been removed. Then the material is heated to complete what the company calls "de-bugging," and sent to the landfill to return to the soil. Reassured, we accepted the pot's convenience. What I really wanted was a composting toilet, but we would have to add that to our wish list for some unidentified time in the future.

We haunted eco-building shows, compiling notes about solar panels, cisterns, green roofs, on-demand water heaters. We saw a pedal-powered grain grinder and joked about all the techno-toys we could get if only David would commit to sustained pedaling. I'm not sure why it was always David who would need to do the pedaling, but it was. Then all of our memos were stored for future use. For the time being we would merely do without. A sort of Third-World living in rural Oregon.

Initially the trailer had a nice spare look, almost a Japanese flavor. I imagine that one person living alone, or even two people who were scrupulous housekeepers—and had virtually no projects or belongings—could have kept it that way. But time and clutter narrowed the already small spaces and passageways. If David and I carefully timed our motions, we could go about our business without bumping into each other. With a three-foot space between the kitchen counter and the cupboards on the other side, when I worked at the counter and David walked by we did a dance: one step forward, one step back, one step forward. Sometimes we moved through the house in a little parade. If a dog or cat happened to be leading the parade, we needed either a great deal of patience or a cattle prod. Often it was "Will you pass me the green tea?" or "The pruners are right behind you. Could you get them for me please?" because it was easier to ask than to try to get around the other person. But fortunately, we never spent much time inside.

When our grandson Nate was about ten, he and his eight-year-old sister, Celina, came to visit. I assumed they'd enjoy sleeping in a tent, but was worried that without TV or computer games Nate would be horribly bored. I was also concerned that seeing his grandparents in such humble straits might make him uncomfortable. But he looked around the trailer and saw the camp stove, the propane heater on the floor, and the lantern hanging overhead; he checked out the battery-operated radio, looked up to the roof, then to the jugs of fresh water lined along the wall and to the foot of the bed just showing from the other room. Finally, he said, "You have everything you need here." I smiled and thought, "No need to worry about this boy being too materialistic!" And then the two of them went out and had a rip-roaring time playing in and around the pond, electronics be damned!

Compared to the hundreds of thousands of homes under bridges, in cars, in cardboard boxes, or in caves, this was a castle, albeit a leaky, drafty, musty, cramped castle. But compared to the American Dream, it was definitely a shack. It felt even more like a shack when its already-old frame got older still and the tip-out started sinking into the ground, opening ever-wider gaps both for the rain above and for cold air and critters from below. When I was telling a friend about our trailer she joked, "Is the roof covered with a blue tarp?"

"No," I told her. It's black plastic."

We stuffed newspapers and rags in the floor cracks (cut-off jeans legs work well). Then we put away David's drafting table. He moved to the desk and I moved to the card table, which also, unfortunately, became the primary repository of piles of bills, work records, magazines, and other homeless paper.

We came to the woods knowing that most of our time would be spent outside, and the trailer would be adequate for those few things that required shelter. But there were many surprises through the years. I wondered one early winter why our clothes were beginning to smell so bad. I knew they were clammy when I got them out of the built-in drawers, but it took a while to realize that drawers against thin exterior walls get and remain damp in Oregon winters. Our clothes were molding. So we emptied the drawers and began storing clothes in piles nearer to the heater. Then, preparing for a rare dressy evening out, I discovered that the elastic waistband in my panty hose had rotted, soon to be followed by anything else elastic in the house. Rusty zippers were next, and I began finding all of my envelopes pre-glued.

So no, this was hardly the American Dream. I never did buy into the American Dream. But then, I can't say I aspired to living in a moldering shack, either.

When we announced our intention to rent out our house in town and camp on our property, people thought we'd lost our minds. Friends worried about us. Acquaintances pitied us. Some reacted with skepticism, doubting our staying power. Others felt scorn that we could find such living acceptable. In retrospect, I understand their confusion and concern. I remember driving through country marred by disreputable little house trailers. I ached for the suffering of the occupants and exclaimed that I could never live in one of those hovels. But even as we did indeed move into one, I refused to acknowledge any kinship with those objects of my pity. Somehow camping here didn't feel like "living in one of those hovels." It was a wayside—a parking spot—in the midst of a journey, not the journey's destination. And isn't that how many of my pitiful compatriots must feel? I've read that as many as 70 percent of lower-income people believe that they will win the lottery, work their way to the top, have their genius recognized and become one of the top 2 percent on America's economic ladder. Perhaps all those ugly little trailers are considered to be brief interludes during the pursuit of the occupants' dreams.

I undoubtedly had some misgivings. I would tell people we were camping, but I rarely confessed it was in a trailer. And I all but stopped inviting friends to visit. I suppose that, deep down, I was afraid someone would pity me, as I had those anonymous trailer-dwellers. Excited as I was about all other aspects of our venture, I would have much preferred awe to pity.

But one exclamation really threw me: "Your husband is an architect! How can he put up with living like that?"

For a moment I had real doubt. I hadn't felt that I was the engine behind this move—that it was all my crazy idea and he was politely going along. But what if that really was the case? So I quoted the skeptics to David and threw in questions of my own. He explained that to him, architecture was about problem solving, not a way of life. He could solve problems in the woods as well as (perhaps better than) he could in town. And this would give him an opportunity to find out what the land might dictate and what he could build to satisfy those dictates.

His response quieted my concerns. And my friend Hannah was supportive as well. Having grown up in New York City, she marveled that I wasn't afraid of the lions and tigers and bears in our new wilderness home. But she seemed intrigued by our venture, and eventually suggested I write about it. So we turned deaf ears to our doubting friends, got out old books on camp cookery, and said good-bye to telephones, television, and electrical appliances. We promised each other we wouldn't waste time and money improving the trailer. We would make do.

Making do wasn't foreign to either of us. Born mid-way between the stock market crash of 1929 and Pearl Harbor, we each came into the world with our mouths far from any silver spoons. During World War II many things were rationed. I remember waiting in long gas lines; my father using saccharine tablets instead of sugar in his coffee; mixing little packets of coloring—which first looked red, then orange, and finally yellow——into bowls of white lard-like margarine, as a substitute for butter; and collecting every available scrap of tin foil, which we rolled into little balls and gave to somebody to use "for the war effort." My big sister and I collected bottles from ditches decades before Oregon's bottle bill, and our whole family recycled, fixed, or reused everything.

My mother's father died in the flu epidemic of 1918, leaving my grandmother and her seven children to scrabble out a living near Missoula, Montana. So Mother learned frugality early. And Daddy's youth, spent on a farm east of the Rockies, near the little Montana town of Valier, had certainly not been opulent. He often spoke of having had only one sweater as a boy (at a time, I suppose) when I was coveting a new turtleneck or cardigan. We learned that "money doesn't grow on trees" and frequently heard Mother deride "conspicuous consumption."

David's experience with long-term camping began prenatally. His parents had spent a couple of years in a tent at Crater Lake while his engineer father helped build the Rim Road. David was conceived in that tent, and his mother returned to civilization only in order to deliver her baby. Through the years his family camped when they traveled. Later he spent the better part of two years in an army tent in Georgia; they burned soft coal to heat the tent and he remembers waking at night to a tent full of green smoke from clogged flues. Someone had to get up to take apart the stove, clean the flues, and set it all back up again. Our venture would be luxurious compared to that.

We began our marriage camping as well, backpacking into Honeymoon Meadows in the Olympic Mountains. We were carrying too much weight, so we cleverly (and I suppose at the time we thought romantically) chose to leave one sleeping bag behind. Our first week of marriage we shared a sleeping bag under the roof of an Adirondack shelter, with the bag open to the breezes on David's side, and mice running back and forth over the top of us. We didn't just endure that week: we exulted in it. It seemed to me that fact alone should bode well for our new adventure.

Fifteen years after we moved to our land I asked David what had been his biggest surprise. He said, "That we could do it."

"You mean you didn't think we could?"

"No. I just thought it would be harder. But it worked. We could live comfortably on much less. And that means less worry. We could separate wants and needs. We could just be."

Chapter Four

Joining us on our trek to a new life were our two dogs, Sadie and Issa, plus our daughter's old cat, McKenzie, and four kittens, found a month before by our six-year-old grand-niece, Janie. Janie longed to have siblings and cousins, and perhaps it was to fill that hole that she brought home stray animals. We inherited the kittens when Kim, Janie's mother, along with their resident cats, declared their allotted space for felines to be filled.

Several years earlier our son Jeff and his wife had met a frantic man in a cookie store, telling of a stray dog he had rescued and the havoc she was raising with his cat. He couldn't keep the dog, but hated to send her to the pound. Unable to allow the dog's probable death, Jeff and M.A. (our name for Jeff's wife, who was officially "Mary Ann") took her in. At that point they had a not-yet-two-year-old son and a baby on the way, along with an older dog who didn't appreciate a bouncy young intruder.

That intruder was Sadie—a black and white, long-eared, long-tailed, high-energy springer spaniel. After a couple of months whirling Jeff's household into a maelstrom, this rowdy sweetheart became ours. Later we got Issa, a half-Dalmatian puppy, as a companion for Sadie, who we could play with all day and tire only ourselves. Issa became Sadie's more than ours, and like a closely spaced second child, relieved us of a good deal of entertainment responsibility. They tussled and played by the hour, and both were ecstatic whenever they came with us on our jaunts to the country.

Concrete blocks boosted the trailer a few feet above the ground. Once the trailer became our home, the dogs claimed the space below it as their domain. With no doors or gates to restrain them, they spent hours chasing and exploring. Appreciating that, unlike in town, no neighbors lived close enough to complain, we quickly learned to sleep through their barking. The dogs' wandering taught us more about our local wildlife than we could have discovered on our own. One time they came home with noses full of porcupine quills (though fifteen years later we had not yet seen a porky). We removed the spines one by one, with fingers or with pliers. Some spots were so tender that it took the two of us to hold the dog still. But even after their miserable ordeal, they felt the need to fraternize with porcupines again—and yet again. Not quick learners, these.

We had seen sign of raccoons and worried that the dogs might tangle with them but they never did, or never that we knew, anyway. They were eager to investigate the countryside and if they were gone more than a few hours we would fret until their return. Once Issa came home half a day after disappearing, but no Sadie. When a day went by, and then another, I was beside myself. Sadie was genetically a bird dog, excited to corner and bark at pheasants, and occasionally other birds, but she was not at all aggressive. Issa was more of a predator, chasing squirrels, cats, and rabbits, and occasionally catching one. I was afraid that together they had chased someone's sheep and Sadie had been shot.

On the third day, she dragged home. There were no shot wounds but her belly was bloody, scratched, and torn. She was a very submissive dog and at the least threat would be on her back. I imagined the dogs had come across a coyote, or a pack of coyotes, and while Issa escaped, Sadie rolled over. I don't know if it would have been coyote behavior to let her live. If she posed no real threat, perhaps teaching her a lesson would have been sufficient.

That was pretty much the end of their long outings, although Issa did take one more amazing journey. One summer we house-sat in Lorane for our friends Donna and George while they were in England. A week or so after they returned and we had moved back to our woods, we came home from town to find Issa gone. We searched and called, and as we came back down the hill where we had been looking, were surprised to see Donna drive up. "Have you lost a dog?" she asked.

"Well, yes. But how did you know?"

"I think we have her."

We drove to Donna and George's house, and sure enough, there was Issa. She had refused to get in Donna's car, but she stayed close to the house. We were dumbfounded. Donna and George lived over six miles from us and we had always driven there. We were incredulous that Issa could have found her way. But obviously, she did.

As the dogs got older we let them come in at night. Two more bodies in the narrow aisles, under the table, or joining us in bed were a bit of a challenge, but we worried about them lost or cold in their old age.

One night when David had already gone to sleep, I "locked" the front door—by pulling a rubber band around the knob and securing it on a nail on the door trim. Just as I blew out the candles and was on my way to bed, I heard the hum of a motor and saw twin light beams piercing the dark driveway. We rarely have visitors, and night visitors to an unlit trailer alarmed me. I watched through the window as three men with rifles got out of their truck, walked around our pickup, and started up the road. Hunters, I supposed, who had no business on our property.

I thought of the old shotgun and rifle that were in the closet, unloaded and certainly rusty, guns that had belonged to my father and grandfather. I fantasized sticking a barrel out the window and, in my best Annie Oakley voice, saying, "You boys better git out of here right now!" But in the middle of my fantasy, Sadie and Issa popped the rubber-band "lock" off its knob and nail and blasted out the door toward the men, barking furiously. Although the dogs could be quite noisy, they were never dangerous. Fortunately, the men didn't know that.

"Dogs!" one shouted.

"Let's get out of here," another said.

They ran for their pickup, gunned the motor and, spinning gravel, roared backwards down the drive. I blessed my canine homeland-security crew.

The cats, too, could be part of the staff if they would help with the mice and voles. McKenzie, our daughter's cat, was a good mouser although she seemed to prefer bringing in snakes and dragonflies. Black, tiny, and fierce as a panther, she quickly had dogs well trained. If a strange dog came within a block of her she would walk deliberately toward it, back low and tail switching. Even large dogs would run away, terrified. She stayed out of trouble and took good care of herself until some time after her nineteenth birthday, when she curled up under a tree and went to sleep for good.

Now we have Caesar, a regal-looking fellow with white bib, black suit, and stubby tail. Also brought to us by our grand-niece Janie, he was born feral and is sweet but ornery, skittery, and unpredictable. Between McKenzie and Caesar were those four kittens who came here when we did. None of them ever reached maturity. What got them I don't know, but we have owls and hawks, raccoons and coyotes, not to mention foxes, bobcats, cougar, and bear. So you've got to be a smart little feline if you're going to get your share of mice in these hills without becoming dinner for someone else. Our Caesar stays safe by hiding in the trailer. Meanwhile Janie has grown up and now has a husband, a baby boy, and a dog of her own.

When I write I often sit by our cluttered card table with a laptop perched on my knees, its plug connected to a one-hundred-foot extension cord, which in turn is plugged into a gas generator stored under a plastic tent as far from the trailer as possible, so that we hear less of its obnoxious noise. The whole set-up would make a good picture for a Far Side cartoon. I prefer to sit on the bed to write but can do that only in the daytime as David goes to bed early and I work mostly at night. First drafts are longhand on a yellow legal pad or the blank backs of junk mail, written outside when possible, or on the bed if the weather or my state of mind excuse me from daylight chores. Otherwise, I work on or beside the table.

Once when I was writing about our primitive life style, I looked up to see a deer mouse standing on its hind feet on the counter, slender paws against a bar of soap, nibbling furiously. Suddenly it turned, tiny obsidian beads staring at me from beneath over-sized translucent ears, its whip-like tail half-again as long as its body, which was no bigger than my thumb. Abruptly it spun around and scuttled behind the Coleman stove, into the fan-housing in the wall, which it could safely share with the long-dormant fan.

"I really do need to do something about the mice," I thought for the five hundredth time. Earlier in the day I'd seen one drowned in a bucket of used dishwater that we were saving for flushing the toilet, and many nights we would fall asleep to squeaking and the rattling of papers in a storage cupboard.

When we decided to move into this trailer, I wasn't prepared for living with mice. We stored our food in plastic and cardboard, our hand-knit sweaters in drawers. It took some time for the mice to discover us, but too soon I was throwing out fouled food and wailing over huge holes shredded as nesting material from precious sweaters knit by our daughter, and one by Hannah for my sixtieth birthday. I set myriad traps baited with peanut butter, so angry at the mice that, initially, killing them seemed justified. But after a few days I began to hate doing it. Once again I had reacted emotionally and violently, just as I had done with the voles. The little creatures were just trying to make a living. Besides, what sense would it make to declare war on them? They could continue invading this dilapidated building as fast as we broke their necks. We would need to mouse-proof the trailer—putting time and money into a structure worthy of neither—or accept our co-habitants.

So I learned to put food in glass and hard plastic, and keep my few remaining sweaters in tight-lidded storage boxes. I protected food-preparation surfaces from little mouse feet and, with the help of a cat, coexisted more or less peacefully with our rodent friends. I thought enviously of the gopher snake Ed Abbey invited into his cabin, keeping his domestic life free from mice. But I doubted our cat would appreciate the help. Now I even find the wee critters amusing occasionally, as they hide stolen cat food in some of my bowls, or boldly chase each other over the tops of the spice jars.

One night I fixed salmon for dinner. I seared the skin-side of a fillet and peeled the skin off, depositing it on butcher paper until after dinner, when I would take it out to the burn barrel. When dinner was over, I got up just in time to see the fish skin disappearing under the front edge of the Coleman stove. "Stop that, you thief!" I yelled, and the skin stopped moving, letting me rescue it while I still could, and saving us from a future of living with its rotting perfume.

Mice are just one of the species blithely uninterested in buying in to our program. Voles eat plants from their roots up, pulling display-garden beauties into their nether chambers; deer eat plants from the top down and, after all these years, still haven't learned the rules of proper pruning. Raccoons, bobcats, and coyotes eat little kittens; birds eat the fertilizer pellets out of the pots; chipmunks devour newly germinated dogwood seeds and nascent lily buds. It seemed we would have many companions on our journey. And it was each species for itself.

Several summers we had mysterious goings-on. Once David had been working in the vegetable garden. At the end of the day he turned the wheelbarrow upside down over fertilizer and hand tools to keep them safe and dry. When he returned in the morning, the fertilizer bag was in the open and was torn and spilled. The next day it was gone, with a little trail of fertilizer going up our driveway and into the brush.

Another day he called to me, "Come check this out!" The tractor seat was in shreds and the tractor's hydraulic line had been pierced.

Later our water pressure suddenly dropped. David and our neighbor Dennis scouted the water line and found fantastic fountains along twenty feet of perforated pipe. This all reached a peak one evening when we arrived home to see Lupi, our visiting granddog, waiting for us on the hood of the '72 Toyota Corolla our son had given us when he bought a new car. She ran to us and proceeded up the driveway very tentatively, urging us to come, but unwilling to get very far ahead of us. Half-way up the road we came to Lupi's big plastic storage container of dog food, on its side, fifteen feet from where we kept it. We picked up the spilled food, put the lid back on, put the carton away and continued up the road. Finally we stopped, looking ahead.

"What's that black lump at the rise in the road?" David asked.

Always the smartass, I answered casually, "Oh, it's a bear." Then I looked again. "My gosh, it *is* a bear."

We four stood and stared at each other for several minutes before the bear turned and ambled off, probably making a mental note to come back for the dog food when it had less company.

I know there are folks who would take joy in bagging a bear, as well as not questioning killing the mice or voles or insects. But we questioned it all. Life is much simpler when you can color things black and white. "Shoot the sonuvabitch!" ranchers I met in eastern Oregon would say, concerning whatever might appear threatening to the rancher, his family, his livestock, or his crops. My father faithfully sprayed for anything likely to damage the roses or the apples. It was the accepted and responsible thing to do. In horticultural studies I learned to spray on schedule rather than for a perceived need—a pre-emptive strike, so to speak.

I remember my father sitting quietly, patiently, with his shotgun trained on a mole hill, just waiting for a wiggle. Then *ka-bluuie*! No more mole. When I came home on vacation my freshman year in college, my family ate delicious venison we called "duck" because it was duck season when the deer helped itself to my parents' prize roses.

My family always knew about beneficial insects—like lady-bugs and honey bees—and we hoped they would stay away on spray day. But the greater good was to get rid of the aphids and thrips, red spider mites, and scale. I remember Canadian scientist David Suzuki saying that in early post-World-War-II days, his conscientious mother would fill the plates for dinner and then spray them with DDT before the family ate. In those days, the new pesticides were considered miracles. No annoying critters need make us sick or harm our crops ever again.

Eventually we learned it wasn't so simple. When insects are sprayed, a small percentage prove to be insensitive to the poison. The resistant bugs mate, producing even-more-resistant offspring. The farmers' usual response is to find another spray. But some thought about organic gardening—which had been the accepted practice before the post-war chemical boom—and began learning to increase fertility and discourage plant pests with more natural methods.

Long before we moved to the Lorane hills, I had sworn off poisons. I had learned that insects become resistant to chemicals, but beyond that, I no longer believed in good bugs and bad bugs. The ones that chew the plants still may be crucial food for birds or other insects, or perhaps they are destined to become butterflies or otherwise charismatic or vital creatures. And in my heart I didn't believe in animal pests either, in spite of getting alternately frustrated and furious at them when they destroyed my plants or belongings.

Because growing and protecting the plants was my job, David was willing to humor whatever kick I was on. He probably would have supported conventional methods if that had been my approach. But even though the animals occasionally made me crazy, I had always considered myself a pacifist and, intellectually at least, that extended to all species. I had never been able to understand people who would vilify whatever or whoever stood in their way. The feeling often seemed to be that my path is the good one, the correct one, so anyone obstructing it must be evil. Trap them. Bomb them. Boo the visiting team.

I was around ten when I first wondered about the concept of good and evil, friend and foe. The radio waves were full of The War: Germany and Japan were evil. Russia and China were our friends. Then, seemingly overnight, Russia was the evil one and Germany was our good pal. That's the first time I remember questioning whether grownups really were as omniscient as I had always thought.

Aleksandr Solzhenitsyn said, "If only it were all so simple! If only there were evil people somewhere insidiously committing evil deeds, and it were necessary only to separate them from the rest of us and destroy them. But the line dividing good and evil cuts through the heart of every human being. And who is willing to destroy a piece of his own heart?"

In the garden, as in international relations, if problems can be traced to their cause and the cause be dealt with, wide-ranging devastation shouldn't be required to control marauding rodents or other offensive creatures. I am no diplomat and wouldn't presume to understand international relations. And the incredibly complex intricacies of an ecosystem are far beyond my ken. But I wonder if in both cases the first step might be to relinquish the idea of control, of dominance, of dominion. Accepting other species, other races, other religions, and ethnicities, accepting that each has a right to pursue and shape its life; perhaps believing in the possibility and rightness of coexistence rather than the necessity for preeminence is the way to start.

And coexistence was a good place for me to begin. Our domestic animals had their own idiosyncrasies (as do we), but they were idiosyncrasies we understood, and they (to a greater or lesser extent) adjusted their habits to fit into our lives. We all—David and I and our animals—plunked ourselves into the midst of wild habitats and relationships, and were distressed when the natives didn't cooperate. These native animals adjusted faster than did their occupiers, taking advantage of soft soil, succulent vegetation, or other temptations we inadvertently offered, but otherwise going about their business and avoiding or ignoring us. They were the innocents, just trying to live their lives. I was the one who had anger in my heart. And isn't it that anger—anger that is willing to kill for ethnicity, for retribution, for ridding the garden of unwanted species—that is the real evil? It was that evil I wanted to learn how to dissolve.

I became determined to talk less and listen more, to be less full of plans and more tuned in to the habits and needs of my wild neighbors. I no longer would try to kill them—but still, I couldn't always tolerate their destructive habits. I needed to go deeper, to pay attention, to search for causes and connections in my future attempts to coexist with my fellow earthlings in our garden and nursery. There had to be something more elegant—and more effective—than merely shooting the sonuvabitch.

Chapter Five

Living in our woods, I seldom want to leave them. David still needs to engage with the world, but I could be a happy hermit. I like to discover new plants and animals and check on those I've already met. I like to watch their changes from season to season and year to year. I want to understand the relationships and connections and how the communities and systems work.

One of my favorite observation spots is the pond. Independent of all our stewing about it—all of *my* stewing; David tends not to anguish about the future; he accepts things as they are—nature gradually adopted the pond. Seeds and eggs transported by the wind and the feet of ducks brought colonies of cattails and rushes, thickets of willows, and even some cottonwoods. Small birds flit through the brush, search for insects in the mud, drink water from pond edges. A kingfisher dives from an old oak branch, rattling as he flies. Raccoons, coyotes, and deer visit for a drink. Roughskinned newts, frogs, and insects swim among water plants, and dragonflies, damselflies, and bats skim the surface.

I've watched assorted critters playing in the pond, two-legged as well as four- and six-legged. Our springer spaniel Sadie loved to swim, her long ears floating on the water. Her buddy Issa was not interested in getting wet and would run back and forth on the bank, looking anxiously at Sadie. Sadie even tried for her regular swim on a cold winter day when the pond had frozen over. After just a few steps, she broke through and found herself trapped, having neither space to swim nor a secure surface to support her weight. Not remembering she had no opposable thumb, I offered her a long pole to grab. After a few panicky moments for both of us, she flailed her way through the ice to the shore. Sadly, she was forever after less eager to swim.

The clay bottom that holds the water has tiny particles that remain in suspension, making for a delightfully gooey, sticky mud. When our older grandchildren, Nate and Celina, were little, they would have mud wars, and paint their bodies, faces, and hair with mud. Later they rafted on the pond, and still later honed their kayaking skills, but by that point they tried to get in and out of the kayak without getting mud between their toes.

One evening I brought my sleeping bag to the pond and decided to make a night of it. When I arrived, ducks took off from the water, beating a double paradiddle with their wings. A light breeze lifted willow leaves, exposing their silvery undersides. The reflection in the pond seemed to paint white blossoms blooming from atop the willows. Cedar waxwings searched for insects above the pond, lighting on a branch, sallying out to snatch a fly, and winging back again to their perch. At night I could barely make out the shadowy figures of bats, helping free my evening of mosquitoes.

I lay on my belly and got a cricket's eye view of the thin and weedy grass. From that angle it looked like a beautiful wildflower meadow: fuchsia-colored vetch, fading vetch in pale blue, tiny yellow clovers, yellow balls that were English daisies without their white ray flowers, white and pink daisies. In the morning minute drops of dew at the tip of each blade of grass shone like jewels. From the right angle the grass blades disappeared and the water droplets were balls of light across the pond.

In the pond's third or fourth year we started to hear strange noises, sometimes like a single note on a tuba, other times like a bass fiddle warming up, and occasionally like tones from a Tibetan throat singer. Being the kind, reassuring grandmother I am, I used to tell Celina that these were the songs of the Pond Monster. I don't remember how we finally found out the musicians were bullfrogs and am equally unsure how they got there. Presumably they had either hopped in over land or been brought in as eggs by visiting birds. I enjoyed listening to them and was distressed to discover that, if I were a conscientious person, I'd arrange to put them all in a big stew.

Bullfrogs are native to the southeast, brought west by someone hoping to market frog legs. Like other exotic species, their natural predators didn't come with them and their population is exploding. They have gluttonous appetites and will eat anything they can get in their mouths, threatening native frogs and young pond turtles. Some restorationists advocate an all-out campaign to capture or kill them. Philosophically, that can be better rationalized than could my misguided battles against mice and voles. But practically, it is equally fruitless. We might feel virtuous and briefly victorious if we waged all-out war, but the bullfrogs arrived in our pond on their own. Even if we dispatched them momentarily, more would soon hop in to take their place. Great blue herons visit the pond occasionally. Perhaps they will acquire a taste for bullfrogs and their tadpoles. Until then I'll appreciate the absence of mosquitoes near the pond, as I listen to frog music and check out recipes for frog legs.

Wandering the property and reading everything I can find on native species, I've learned some of the contributions made by our so-called pests. Those wretched voles that wiped out our display garden, along with the rabbits, chipmunks, and other rodents who eat seedlings, flower buds, and new plant growth, are all vitally important food for hawks and owls.

After our ill-fated attempt to gas the voles, it occurred to me that they doubtless have an important role in enriching the soil as well. I had recently taught a class in composting and the more I thought about it, the more it seemed I had a crew of little compost makers hard at work. First the voles would help aerate the soil, mixing layers as they tunneled through. Then they would pull vegetation into their tunnels, eating and digesting part and scattering the rest about. The plant material and feces would attract millipedes, slugs, and worms to shred and digest it, and also attract their predators—centipedes, beetles, and ants. The whole crew would eat, excrete, reproduce, and die, adding to the organic material in the soil that would finally be decomposed by fungi and bacteria. After those microorganisms died or were eaten by protozoans and nematodes, their stored nutrients would be released to the soil to be available for new plants. Other herbivorous tunneling rodents certainly play a similar role, along with many ants and earthworms. Perhaps not the method of adding organic matter to the soil espoused by the gardening books, but effective.

Insects and spiders inhabit fascinating niches. Many are important food for birds or frogs. Some are eaten by other insects that are then eaten by the birds or frogs. Various flies, wasps, beetles, and gastropods (slugs and snails) are the first line of defense against our being buried in the carcasses and waste of mammals, reptiles, spiders, and insects, along with countless tons of cast-off plant debris. These creatures break down nature's garbage, beginning the essential cycle of decomposition. Many insects—not just honey bees—are pollinators, and without them there would be far fewer fruits or seeds.

Garden wasps nearly defeat me some summers. Both yellow jackets and black wasps build their nests in the ground and I frequently disturb them when I'm weeding or pruning. Unlike honey bees, they are aggressive and territorial and don't even give you the satisfaction of dying when they sting. I'm not dangerously sensitive but I do react to their venom and besides, it bloody *hurts*. I do know that they are pollinators so I forgive them some of their sins, as long as they keep their distance. But, since watching them at work, I've learned to respect—if not love—them.

One summer morning we found the plump body of a vole lying in the path, probably a victim of the cat. As we watched, a couple of yellow jackets lit on it, quickly joined by several more. Soon the body was covered with hungry wasps, and in just a few hours, the bones were clean. We've witnessed similar routines several times since then. We heard a story about a woman who had baited live-traps with fish heads in order to remove some unwelcome four-footed guest from her garden. By the end of the day the wasps had devoured the bait and the intended captive had not been near.

Some months later we saw the next strand of the great web. A football-size hole had been excavated beside the driveway, and lining the hole were remnant scraps of wasp larval cells. Scattered yellow jackets were busily working to rebuild their ravished nest, but within a few days, they were gone as well. Skunks eat wasps, as do bears, but there was no sign of the perpetrator. Several summers after that, we saw a number of these distinctive holes, all appearing within a couple of weeks of a bear's visit. We've not seen any skunks yet, but we've smelled a few. And we have learned not to store dog food or other irresistible comestibles outside— not because we might lose them to the bears or other wild things, but because teaching the creatures to come close to human dwellings for food will ultimately threaten the life of the animal. Our new motto is, "Let them eat wasps!"

I am not one who looks forward to the "peaceable kingdom." I think the lion will lie down with the lamb when, as in the paintings of ancient Romans, she finds that the most comfortable position for dining, and I think that is as it should be. The more I learn, the more I appreciate the full range of creatures. I feel a tremendous kinship with the mammals that I get a chance to watch. In their behavior and expressions, I see my own feelings. In birds, invertebrates, and microorganisms I see the engineers that bring balance to this world.

I love learning about creatures' niches, seeing how each is important to the functioning of an ecosystem. But eventually I realized that healthy interactions among the diverse species make my job immeasurably easier as well. Weed control, insect control, soil fertility, moisture retention, all are greatly simplified as the garden comes closer to balance.

So I try to stay out of the critters' way and let them do their job. At the same time, I try to understand their habits well enough to protect our plants. Deer must be fenced out of the nursery. A nurseryman friend of ours once commented that deer wouldn't be a problem "except for too few cougars and too damned many vegetarians." But because we have introduced our nursery to their land—and we're not into venison—it's our responsibility to keep susceptible plants out of their reach. Ditto the rodents. Those coldframes and flats of succulent newly germinated seedlings must be screened top and bottom with wire mesh. I must get rid of places where the chipmunks can hide from hawks and owls, to eat plants uninterrupted. The trick, I think, is to try to be as smart as the animals are. If I scatter temptations about, I'd best not be annoyed when they accept them. And I must strive for balance so natural cycles prevail. I think I'll budget in an intentional tithe for the critters as well.

In his need to connect with the world, David takes occasional jaunts into the little community of Lorane to join whatever locals are assembled for breakfast or lunch. Now and then, I join him. We descend Easy Acres Drive (a misnomer if I ever heard one—I'd name it Hard Scrabble Road), and turn south on Territorial Highway. Territorial was the main north-south road for pioneers, and before that, a trade route and footpath for the Kalapuyas. When the white settlers came it became known as Halo Trail, for Chief Halo (called Camafeema by his people). Eventually it became the Oregon Trail of Tears, because it was along this route that southern Oregon Indians, forced on foot to reservations in the north, suffered heartbreak, sickness, and death. Later it served as a stagecoach road, and was popular for horseback, buggies, and foot traffic. Once settlers began using cars they found themselves mired in the mud during the rainy season. Some sections were laid with planks, three wide ones on each side, nailed over cross boards.

East of Territorial is Coyote Creek and an extensive wetland. The foothills of Oregon's Coast Range rise quickly to the west. We pass Jackson-Marlow and Ham roads and then begin an upwards serpentine. Now the hills are steep to the east and fall away from the highway to a narrow valley on the west before climbing again into the foothills. In July we travel by a hillside blushing pink, covered with *Clarkia*, the appropriately named farewell-to-spring. We drive over the collapsing and oft-mended road where run-off from the hill above gathers soil particles, turning the ground beneath the road to liquid mud that flows down the hill. Soon we crest Stoney Point, the divide between the Long Tom and Siuslaw watersheds. Poised at its summit we look out to wide-open fields, pastures, and, nestled on a bordering hill ahead, the castle-like complex that is King Estate winery. We drop into the valley and soon reach Lorane. The distance we cover is only six miles on the odometer, but rich in scenery and diversity.

On the main road, the unincorporated community of Lorane consists of a post office and two stores—one with gas pumps and the second at a three-way intersection: Territorial curving to Drain and I-5, Siuslaw River Road to the coast, and a road that leads to Cottage Grove, twenty miles to the west. A block above, on Old Lorane Road, stand a church, a fire station, an elementary school, the grange, and the Odd Fellows and Rebekah Lodge.

The locals are an eclectic mix of old-timers, loggers, hunters, New-Agers, Christians, artists, and urban transplants. The Lorane General Store holds a deli and a lot of history. That's where David goes for local companionship and an occasional meal. The General Store is on the site of the first business in Lorane, built in 1888. Even then it was a gathering place. There are stories of men circled around the pot-bellied stove, sharing yarns and coffee, or eating a lunch of sardines, crackers, and hunks of Tillamook cheese. The original store was moved and then burned down. The current store was built in 1938.

We cross a broad front porch with a long bench and tables and chairs for sunny-weather eating. Inside we walk wide uneven floorboards, oiled dark, alongside an open kitchen divided from the customers by cases of pies, cakes, salads, and quiche. In the back of the room the focal point is a heavy rectangular cast-iron stove on a raised brick platform. On cold or rainy days customers blow in, wet from logging, mushroom hunting, or just walking from their car to the store. Folks head straight for the stove, rubs hands together, then turn to warm backs and greet friends.

David and I like to sit at a round communal table near the stove and beside a defunct door burned with cattle brands. In the center of the table are reading glasses of various strengths. On the wall are coffee cups, and on a nearby counter, coffee, hot water, and assorted envelopes of tea. Help yourself. One September day we joined Leo, a rasty old six-foot

Dutchman who owned the store; Ken, Crow High School's first graduate; an old logger; a retired teacher; a community college student celebrating her new Pell grant; and Betty, a single mom no one knew. Ken is part Indian as are, he says, most of the long-time locals. Linda, Leo's ex-wife, cooked as she received barbs from Leo and threw back her own. They seemed to have established a comfortable relationship of friendly fighting. Leo worried about the stock market, discussed his investments, told a story about sailing solo around Washington's San Juan Islands on his way to Anacortes when he ran out of wind. Ken interrupted, "Leo, you're never out of wind." His sails are down now, though. A couple of years after that lunch, Leo was killed by skin cancer.

The deli is the daily heart beat of Lorane, but seasonally the community throbs on Old Lorane Road on the hill above. Begun as a fund-raiser for a local family in need, an annual ice-cream social the second Sunday of each August now benefits the volunteer fire department. People gather at the fire station for homemade ice cream and pie, while children, supervised by uniformed firemen, have hose-drenching contests, play water ball, jump in dunk tanks, and take rides in the fire truck's cherry picker.

For many years, Lorane women spent two days in the week before Thanksgiving at the Grange baking pumpkin pies that they sold as a benefit for Meals for Seniors. We made a habit of ordering two pies and enjoyed picking them up amidst tables covered with flour, pie dough, pies ready to be filled, cans of pumpkin, and aproned women with tired, smiling faces powdered with flour.

We particularly appreciate the monthly Movie Night, first Saturdays through fall and winter. Organized by the Rural Art Center, the evening includes food, socializing, door prizes, local talent, and short films, along with the feature. Proceeds go to local projects, charities, or community groups, including various school projects, a writing group, and the Cottage Grove Humane Society.

The annual Easter beer hunt is not in one of the community buildings, but on the grounds of a local artist. We have not yet attended, but keep promising ourselves a chance to meet the Beer Bunny.

Not only do humans seem genetically wired for community, so too do other primates. E. O. Wilson tells of an experiment in which a monkey would repeatedly pull a lever with its only reward being a glimpse at another monkey. Based on a recent study, some sociologists theorized "belongingness" was the greatest human need beyond basic life necessities.

For such a small population, Lorane does an exemplary job of community building. We are always welcomed. People are warm and generous. But I can't pretend we belong. We enjoy the people, the change, the activities. Then we return home and find our "belongingness" in the woods.

Chapter Six

I tried to scootch down into the garbage can of sun-warmed pond water. It made me giggle to think of bathing in the water we had stored here for irrigating our plants—one of three thirty-two-gallon cans spread about the area where we keep our container plants—but it was warm and lovely and it was calling to me. Big enough to be helpful for watering, it was too tall and narrow for a successful soak. At just under thirty inches high, it nearly matched my inseam, making it a challenge to coax my legs over the edge to get in. Once in, I banged my knees on the sides of the can each time I tried to lower my body into the water. For a while I just stood there, my legs enjoying the bath, my mind delighting in the outrageousness of it all. Then, with apologies to any and all observing birds and squirrels, I heaved my right leg over the tall rim, pointed my toes to reach the ground, and wobbling on tip-toes, yanked and strained until I finally pulled my dripping left leg over the edge to join the right.

So that hadn't worked as a bathtub, but it might serve for face and arm washing, or for a shampoo. I have a friend who once had an old claw-footed tub out in a field when she lived without electricity. It's a romantic picture, but we'd promised ourselves no unnecessary expense, and unfortunately didn't have any spare claw-footed tubs.

Old habits die slowly. After a day's hard and dirty work, for years I reflexively headed for a hot shower. *Oh phooey! No shower.* So I put on a kettle to warm water for soaking cold hands and feet, to make a compress for tired muscles and joints, or to wash away the sweat and grime. My friend Hannah gave us a solar shower as a trailer-warming present (wetting present?) and we have really appreciated a shower when the weather is clear enough to warm the water. The outdoor shower is refreshing and the notion of our past-middle-age bodies naked in the yard is titillating in that same socially unaccepted way as my garbage-can bath. But when the weather doesn't cooperate, sponge baths do the trick, or sponging off friends, plus taking advantage of the gym membership we got as much for the showers as for the exercise. After a few seasons we accepted being without a functioning bathroom inside our humble home, and adapted to alternatives.

Perhaps the most essential ingredient of adaptation is lowering your standards, which is probably easier for someone like myself, brought up with a very small water tank behind the wood cooking range. When I was a child we had no shower and our baths were about two inches deep to be sure the hot water didn't run out. However, we did take daily baths and I was definitely raised in a "cleanliness is next to godliness" society. So I had to acknowledge being a tad defensive when I cut out an article by an internist listing ailments "ranging from contact dermatitis to fungal rashes" caused by daily bathing. He explained that too much washing eliminates beneficial bacteria—"normal flora"—that protect the skin. I was happy to count myself among those dedicated to preserving the normal flora.

Our plan to use pond water for drip irrigation faltered when we realized that our soil's colloidal clay, which our young grandchildren loved using as body paint, would clog the drip emitters unless we changed filters multiple times daily. And we had always understood that watering a whole nursery from our shared well would be out of the question. So, before we moved to the land we hauled water from our house in town. We bought fifty-gallon drums once used for honey, lined them up in the bed of our pick-up and filled them with a garden hose. Our daughter, Erika, spent hours one hot summer working a hand pump that she screwed onto the drums to fill gallon jugs, which she would then carry to the plants. Sometimes she even had to drive back to town for re-fills. The system was slow and inefficient—you might say archaic. It took the better part of every day, with her toil relieved only by an occasional skinny-dip in the pond.

Eventually we bought a three-hundred-gallon tank designed to fit in the back of a pickup, complete with cut-outs to fit over the wheel wells. We filled that in town for a few months, which took a good half-hour using our garden hose. Finally we were able to eliminate the drive to town, thanks to a three-horse-power gas pump that pulls pond water through a one-and-a-half-inch polyethylene pipe to fill the truck-bed tank in less than eight minutes. Then David (usually) drives to the top of a rise near our container-plant enclosure, parking sufficiently high to let gravity fill our water lines, which have apertures large enough to allow for the suspended clay. We hitch a hose to the end of the pipe, and with a watering wand and nozzle at its end, I water each pot by hand. An impressive layer of sludge builds up in the bottom of the tank so I must be careful not to drain it low enough to pull muck into the lines. David checks the pump regularly to guard against the ravages of both mud and of bears. All of which is a bit more complicated than if we'd been able to use drip irrigation—but it's immeasurably better than hand-pumping into gallon jugs!

When we first moved to the nursery we filled jugs for our domestic water supply from a faucet at the house of the next-door neighbor with whom we share a well. After a while we strung 200 feet of PVC pipe from their house to ours but someone (remembering the munched pond liners in clients' yards, we blamed it on raccoons) chewed the lines, and besides that we had some storm breakage. We went back to filling jugs from an outlet near the pump house on the neighbor's property, and continued even after we replaced the ravaged line, whenever we thought the pipes might freeze or otherwise be damaged.

We tried to use as little water as possible. We practiced tough love on our plants, then after a few years switched from a full menu of perennials to focus on native plants, all adapted to the local rhythms of temperature and moisture. We recycled water we used inside and discovered we could get along on considerably less than we might have expected. The local water board reported that the average household use for 2.34 people was 5490 gallons a month in winter, and 17,490 gallons in the summer. We two used about 100 gallons a month in winter and 3100 when we irrigated. Of course that didn't count the water we used at the laundromat or the gym or occasionally at the house of a friend.

Basic conservation methods were not hard in our situation. Leaving the tap running is not an issue when there's no water in the tap, and we flushed the toilet with used dishwater. A friend praised the efficiency of her dishwasher. Doing dishes only when the machine is full saves water, she claimed, and good hot water guarantees cleanliness. Well, I had a dishwasher too. Its name was David. We had enough dishes to last two days, so that's how often the dishwasher needed to operate. On the rare occasions that I washed dishes, I scoured them with a dampened and slightly soapy scrubby. Pouring boiling rinse water over them ensured their sanitation, using between a gallon and two gallons of water for a pan full of dishes. I didn't checked to see how David did it. I'm not very mechanical and I theorized that if I should try to re-program a functioning dishwasher, it might cease to function. I was not willing to take that chance.

I loved the inconvenience of having to carry water. It was a constant reminder to use as little as possible, to re-use when we could, to dump anything we couldn't use ourselves onto plants or soil to help re-charge the groundwater, and to appreciate water as not only vital, but as a blessing. I must confess, I might have loved it less if David hadn't done most of the carrying, but even so, I will never again consider water to be merely an entitlement.

I can still hear how my mother's voice would call, "Don't waste water, Evelyn," as I gazed at the twisting liquid spiraling its silver strands from the faucet. A turn to the right and it disappeared. Turn back to the left and there it was again. Surely it was enchanted! I could look at the small water tank and understand that hot water was limited, but I could see no comparable problem here. Clearly this was a magic faucet.

Global water worries are hard to appreciate in soggy-wintered western Oregon. The United Nations reports that 2.7 billion people will face severe water shortages by 2025. Today, approximately 1.2 billion drink unclean water. More than five million die annually from water-related diseases such as cholera and dysentery. Everywhere farmers and cities pump groundwater faster than it can be replenished. The land surface is dropping in California's Central Valley due to the depletion of aquifers. The Colorado River barely makes it to the Gulf of California; some years the Rio Grande dries up before it reaches the Gulf of Mexico. Numerous small rivers are dry.

People lucky enough to have sufficient clean water tend to take it for granted, just as I did as a child. My mother had no such illusions, having grown up in Montana where water was not plentiful, and having to pump what she needed from a well. It was many years before I realized that the fresh water supply is finite and what we have now (for six and a half billion people and growing) is the same amount we had when people numbered in the thousands—and before there were people at all. To those who have inadequate water, it is the most precious resource in the world, and if they can't get clean water, they'll use what they have, even if it's horribly polluted.

I've been seriously thirsty only once that I can remember, and then briefly, but it was enough that I can imagine a little what it must be like to be without. My experience came during and after a lovely night sleeping on the dike between Malheur and Harney lakes in eastern Oregon. Some folks at the field school I was attending dropped me off there, with a sleeping bag and presumably some food and water, although I don't remember any of either.

Eastern Oregon's skies stretch nearly unbroken from horizon to horizon, and the air feels clean and dry. Shadows move along the barren hills when occasional clouds drift by. Hawks and golden eagles soar on the thermals. I lay in my sleeping bag watching birds and cloud shadows and then saw the black ball of a storm cloud, rolling in my direction. It was a unit—a thing—appearing quite solid as it surged nearer to me. I ducked my head inside the bag as the black cloud billowed by, depositing only a few drops. Most of them evaporated before they hit the ground. My bag wasn't even damp.

A group of mule-deer galloped just feet from my head—which probably wouldn't have been so exciting if they'd been much closer. Overhead, I was treated to a most wonderful aerial ballet when hundreds of white pelicans flew above the lakes in formation, several abreast in long lines, back and forth and around and around as if choreographed. The air was full of the huge white birds who continued their display for an amazingly long time—perhaps a half hour.

Eventually, I got very thirsty. I ran out of water and felt foolish I hadn't brought more. (Just one overnight, after all. How much can you need?) My tongue began to feel thick and my mouth was cottony. I tried to move my tongue to stimulate some saliva. I could hardly pull it loose. I kept looking at the lake water—polluted, I knew. I tried to concentrate on my surroundings—the stars, the clear fresh air, the breeze in the marsh plants. Finally, I slept a bit and awoke barely able to swallow. I headed for the lake. Risking a disease was better than enduring this thirst. I wet only my lips and mouth, not really drinking it—or at least not much. But I understand how thirsty people would drink even dirtier water, if that were all that was available.

Water is not only often fouled, it is becoming increasingly inaccessible. Companies buy water rights and sell the life-giving liquid to the highest bidder. Corporations and resorts may have plentiful water while poor people scramble for a modicum. Water has been called the new oil, both as a source of profit and a cause of war. Inequalities are severe and growing more so. I heard a radio report about a resort in Africa where wealthy vacationers could be heard laughing and splashing, diving and playing in a sparkling blue pool, while just outside, women passed by carrying jugs of water on their heads, having made a journey of several kilometers to get water of questionable purity.

I am reminded of an un-funny cartoon that asked, "Why are most of our immigrants from places we like to vacation?"

I rarely mention to acquaintances that we carry water to the house and drag a hose of pond water for the plants. I hope I'm not embarrassed. When I remember pictures of children getting their only water from what they can wring out of rags they have dipped in mud puddles, it would be more reasonable for me to be self-conscious about the riches of clean water and a pond.

I recently learned that there may be additional benefits from our well water. For each of the myriad bacteria there is a phage, a virus that keeps the bacterium in check. In any spoonful of natural water there are thousands of bacteriophages, which are killed or filtered out of city water. Scientists are trying to harness this potential. They want to use phages as specific antibiotics—a way to control a pathogenetic bacterium without damaging the beneficials. But they haven't done it yet. Meanwhile, we have free access to this natural disease prevention.

We may be avoiding another modern problem as well: respiratory allergies and asthma have been increasing throughout the industrial countries. One hypothesis suggests that too much sanitation has deprived our immune systems of disease-fighting cells. David and I rarely get a cold. Can we credit our antibody-stimulating primitive life style? Too much sanitation is clearly not a concern here.

PART TWO

Spring

Chapter Seven

Well before spring arrives in our hills, I begin to count the signs of its approach. Leaf buds swell on woody branches as early as December. By February clusters of tiny lavender-to-purple bells of snow queen pop up singly and in colonies on the forest floor. They are soon joined by golden chains of filbert catkins and osoberry's hanging bells.

"The girls are out!" exclaimed my field-botanist friend Danna one early March when a group of us were gathered at her house. We all tumbled out to see for ourselves because, though we were all "plant people," many of us had never before seen the tiny ruby-colored female flowers of the filbert. Every year since then, as the filbert catkins stretch, I anticipate the maturing of their pollen that will signal the emergence of "the girls." So minute are the glowing jewels, they seem a private gift. Each time I find one is a thrill, and each time I am reminded of Danna.

A few weeks after the flowering of the filbert, while the snow queen is still blooming, perky four-petaled spring beauty carpets the ground in pink, white flowers crown wild strawberry plants, fans of Oregon iris push through the moss, and willows flaunt their fuzzy, gray flower buds.

Throughout the winter I get a rush from seeing the intense red, yellow, burgundy, and amber stems of willow, vine maple, and red-twig dogwood. Almost at the stroke of March's equinox, those glowing hues begin to dim and softer tones spread across the palette. Alder trees become a rosy haze near creeks and rivers. New leaves emerge in the gentlest of tones: apple green, bronzy green, gray-green, dusty rose. I have read the names Native Americans gave the various moons of the year—evocative names such as Green-corn moon, Big-famine moon, Moon-when-the-calves-grow-hair. It has inspired me to do some naming myself, as each month conjures up different images. I think I would call the moon of new spring the Innocence Moon.

The flying signs of spring also begin right around the equinox. One sunny spring day I was rounding the bend toward the nursery where the drive follows the toe of the hill from the south to the east side, when a huge shadow floated over my head, followed by another from the opposite direction. I looked up to see four turkey vultures doing an aerial quadrille not fifteen feet above me. One would fly south while another went north until reaching the edge of some invisible pre-determined circle, and while they were arcing around to the east and west, the vultures in those positions would pass each other in the center and float to the north and south. I watched in awe, mixed with a certain unease, for a while. Though I was pretty sure I was still alive, it felt as though I were their pivotal point. Eventually I began walking again and they turned unhurriedly away, their great ghostly shadows flickering over the trees, rising and falling. A few steps later my nostrils crinkled to the smell of something dead. I didn't go investigate but I must have been nearly on top of it. I certainly wouldn't have been able to pick up the scent from far above the tree tops.

Turkey vultures are often more than two feet long, and their wingspan can be greater than five and a half feet. They return early from their winter's migration, and I look forward to seeing that distinctive black, shallow V-form in the sky, rocking gently from side to side. Up close they're a bit sinister looking. A naked red head and neck make it easier for them to go carcass-diving without fouling their feathers. Gathering around their carrion feast, they rip meat with strong beaks, often holding it down with one foot. Without the insulation provided by feathers, their naked legs could overheat. So in order to provide evaporative cooling, such as we have with our sweat glands, vultures whitewash their legs with their own excrement. Majestic in flight, at work on the ground they need to be appreciated for the importance of their job rather than for their majesty.

The red-flowering currant is in full bloom by equinox. A pale pink form grows on the south side of the property and a dark red one near the entrance. I've taken cuttings and purchased bare-root plants from wholesale nurseries but never seem to have enough for nursery customers. Next I'll try seed, which shouldn't be difficult—at least the birds know how to get it to germinate, judging from all the seedlings around.

Just as the currants begin to flower, rufous hummingbirds return from their winter migration. They hover, seeking nectar from the drooping blossoms, and squabble with each other. Their wings move in a fast figure-eight motion, whirring as they fly backward, forward, or from side to side. They poke long tongues deep into the sweet nectaries of tubular flowers, lapping nectar, which travels up tiny grooves along the length of their tongues. As a bird moves from blossom to blossom, the flower's anthers deposit pollen on a specific spot on the hummer's head, increasing the chance that the bird will pollinate the next currant even if it laps nectar from a different species along the way.

The males arrive first, scouting to find territory with good food that is likely to attract a multitude of females. Once they stake out their domain, they fiercely protect it from other males. Highly polygamous, they will mate with as many females as possible but take no part in raising the young. The female chooses a breeding ground based on the security of nesting sites and she too drives away all competitors. Extremely aggressive, she has been documented confronting hawks, crows, and jays. Some species of hummingbird will share a feeder, but the rufous *whirs* and *chips* and *zee-chuppity-chups* as it flies at any aspirant to the table.

A friend of mine bans hummers from her garden because of their aggressive behavior, but I admire their brilliant iridescent colors and love watching their aeronautic feats. Plus I appreciate that they're pollinating plants and controlling insect explosions. They perch on posts in my garden or on bare twigs and look for flying insects, which they zip out and capture. Sometimes they hover amid an insect swarm and take as many as thirty in one session, according to the books. I've seen them hanging seemingly still, but with wings whirring near tree trunks and branches, picking bugs and bug eggs from cracks in the bark. One rufous hummingbird was spotted making repeated runs at a mass of aphids for a full twenty minutes. An amazing foraging method I've read about—but not yet observed—is their leaf-blower imitation. They fluff up leaves on the forest floor with gusts of air from their propeller-wings, and then glean insects and their eggs from the undersides of the leaves.

For several years a hummingbird has built her nest in the fir tree immediately above my potting bench. When she's nesting, she hums and dive bombs until, generally, I accede to her demands and take my work elsewhere. It took me a long time to locate the nest. Finally I spotted it on a low branch maybe ten feet off the ground. A cup so tiny it would fit in a child's curled fingers, it was camouflaged with lichen, twigs, and pieces of bark, appearing like little more than a lump on the branch. Though I couldn't have known, looking at it from the ground, she makes her nest from soft things like thistle down, dandelion fluff, hair, or feathers, plus little bits of bark and roots, and binds them together with caterpillar silk and spider webs. Around more civilized dwellings than ours, she might collect lint from dryer flues or use bits of carpet or other fabric fibers. One day I hope to be lucky enough to watch her build.

By or before spring's dawn, many migratory birds return to their Willamette Valley breeding sites—swallows, waxwings, and evening grosbeaks, along with the turkey vultures, rufous hummingbirds, and others. At the same time, the silky silver willow buds of February and March metamorphose to fat, hairy, green and yellow caterpillars whose pollen-laden anthers radiate out, sailing pollen grains in the wind to waiting willow stigmas as well as to the tender eyes and noses of allergy sufferers.

One early April morning I awoke feeling dreadful. My head throbbed, my stomach swirled, and my spirits were flat. How could I possibly do all the work I'd scheduled for the day? The answer was obvious: I couldn't. Staying in bed was just as unappealing. *You've got eternity to rest,* I thought. *Use the excuse to go exploring!* I didn't feel like eating, but I sipped a cup of tea, pulled on my jeans, sweatshirt and hiking boots, and headed up our hill.

There are places so steep on the east side of the hill that I couldn't stand. I grabbed the strong fern fronds to hold myself upright when I could; other times I gave in and crawled on all fours. I traveled through dense sword ferns, with spring beauties and an occasional trillium or patch of fawn lilies between them. At the top of the hill I discovered anemones—pretty little wind flowers I didn't know were there. And then—what's this? My heartbeat quickened as I came upon a huge colony of calypso orchids. I'd have been thrilled to find just one, but this was almost unbelievable. Calypsos are beautiful little rose-purple slipper orchids that I had always thought required old-growth forests. Here they were growing very happily in our second-growth trees. Maybe it's appropriate that I'd never seen them before—*calypso* means "concealment" (inspiring the name of Homer's nymph, hiding in the woods and found by Ulysses)—but I'd never taken the time to find them during this busy season. The climb, the focus, and the necessary deep breathing had diminished my headache to an ignorable residue. The thrill of the calypso colony lifted my spirits to face the day.

Before the end of March I must admit once again how many things I had meant to do during the winter I had not done. I'm already behind when the season really kicks off in early April with the Hardy Plant Society of Oregon plant sale. It's held in Hillsboro, southwest of Portland, in a barn of a fairgrounds building and it brings together seventy or more vendors with thousands of plant-hungry customers. We make two trips, hauling a truckload of plants each time and storing the first load in the side yard of some friends. We spend several days writing each plant's name on narrow white plastic labels, its price on blue ones. Then I lose a few nights' sleep making large labels with pictures I've photocopied from magazines or books, along with cultural information for each species. Soon with heads abuzz, high on adrenaline, caffeine, and the energy of the scene, we are talking plants with enthusiastic customers.

During the three-day sale we arrange plants, re-stock what sells, and count pots, to be sure we'll get the remaining plants home in one load. We speculate what to do if we're left with too many plants: Do we stack them and risk breaking tender stems? Do we leave them in our friends' yard and make yet another trip to retrieve them? Fortunately, we've never had to deal with this problem, but that doesn't keep us from worrying, each time.

On Friday and Saturday nights we stay with our friends. I exult that they have a shower, and joyously run up their water bill. A shower is a lovely thing; I will never again take one for granted. Sunday afternoon we head for home to get ready for more hauling and selling, at Eugene's Farmers' Market plus two other big spring sales.

For eighteen years, Saturdays from April to mid-October—and later Tuesdays as well—found one of us with our plants at the Farmers' Market. In the early years Erika was the salesperson, eventually passing the job on to her parents. It is my job to put together our offerings. I search the growing grounds for plants at their prime. *What is the most showy, the most enticing? Will these blossoms begin to open by tomorrow?* For several years I would get together a truckload, later, after we bought a used van, a vanload—fifteen to twenty flats, each one holding eight one-gallon pots or eighteen to twenty four-inch pots. Gather the plants. Scrub the pots. Check for weeds. Groom the plants. Snip fading flowers, discolored leaves, errant twigs. *You can't go to town looking like that!* Fuss, turn, admire. Then I catch a peek of my dirt-stained fingernails, my soiled, cracked skin and think, "Too bad no one takes time to groom the groomer."

Because he's more gregarious than I and not as impatient spending the day sitting, the market became mainly David's schtick. But track season is spring and summer as well. As head field-communication official for UO track meets, David organizes and oversees a crew that reports information from the various field events (pole vault, shot put, high jump etc.) to the meet announcer. There is no way he'd rather spend a spring Saturday than working a track meet. So whenever there was one scheduled, market duty was mine.

The six-fifteen a.m. arrival time and subsequent booth set-up is a mad dash. I pray that another truck is not parked where I need to be. *Rats! There is!* Park as close as possible. *Hustle!* Unload pipes, fittings, canvas for the shelter. Unload flats of plants, setting them in a neighbor's space to give me room to set up the display shelving that rides in the van under the flats. *Hustle!* Set up shelving. Quickly move flats before neighbors, Ruby and Amber, arrive. *Oops! Here they come.* They need to park where I am. Move van around the corner. Run back. Move flats out of Ruby and Amber's space so they can get to work. Dash back to the van to move it from metered parking to over-park. Now set up the booth with so many flats of plants in my way I can barely move.

Shrubs and trees go in the back, flowering plants in front. Coordinate the colors: yellow, gold, orange, scarlet, with a dash of indigo; separate the pinks, purples, and blues. Check foliage textures: put lacy next to solid. Keep the red-flowering currant and vine maple apart, as well as the ninebark: the leaf shapes are too similar. Check results from all angles. Is it gorgeous? Is it enticing?

Vendors on each side hurriedly replay the same series of actions: Try to park near. Hustle hustle. Set up shelter. Make displays irresistible. I heard a neighbor muse, "The problem is, you make it perfect to look at, then somebody buys something and it ruins the display!"

Finally ready for the onslaught, I sit back to watch and listen. People arrive in bike clothes, long dresses and running shoes, overalls, slip tops and tiny shorts. They wear or carry backpacks, mesh bags, straw bags, bike bags. They push strollers and baby buggies with baskets under, behind, or beside, or roll in wheelchairs with baskets on their laps. I think of our then three-year-old granddaughter, Camila, exclaiming, "Too much people!" as she maneuvered, knee-high, among adult legs at a popular festival.

Mostly the people come for produce, not plants. The fragrance of basil perfumes the air. Stacks of beets, carrots, deep red-skinned potatoes, baskets of cauliflower, broccoli, spinach, beans, and lettuce tempt even the most steadfastly carnivorous customers. Nearby are the "Best-priced tomatoes in the market. Buy two baskets and we'll heap 'em up." Booths boast strawberry, raspberry, apple and blackberry pies; bouquets, blueberries, and tall lilies.

The day includes forums, demonstrations, speeches, and marches. A little girl, about eight years old, stands alone in the closed-off street (might that be her mother hovering in the audience?). Before her is an up-turned hat to receive contributions, and she belts out "Somewheeerre over the rainbow ..." On the corner a local favorite, Eagle Park Slim, sits with guitar case open, strumming, blowing a kazoo and singing, "Back to Eugene where the Grass is Green" and "I've Got the Market Blues." On the next block, the drums begin.

Among the parade of passing produce shoppers I counted on an occasional friend and a few welcome plant customers. I was often visited also by a homeless woman, a market regular. "Could you do something for a poor old woman? I really need a massage and I don't have any money. Nobody cares. I really need a massage and nobody cares."

One Saturday a young African-American boy in shiny over-sized running shorts and jacket approached me shyly. "Would you like to buy a packet to help pay my way to the Junior Olympics in Des Moines, Iowa?" He offered me a book of coupons for local businesses I would probably never patronize, but I couldn't resist him.

Before long it would be four-thirty and time to take everything down, pack it up, and head for home, to get ready to do it all over again next time. So went most of our spring, a little bit of fall, and the entire summer.

In between market days and working in people's yards, potting, weeding, and propagating took most of my spring. If David was not working a track meet he'd be hauling plants to the container compound from my potting area, putting up fences, mowing, or cutting brush. He loves to make oases of calm in the midst of chaos—clearing blackberries from around a single oak tree, cleaning off his desk even if it's the sole empty surface in the house (what was on the desk often ends up in a bag, or in a pile on the card table), raking leaves from a spot on the driveway. Once I watched him raking and thought how content and contemplative he looked. He reminded me of a fellow I read about whose idea of Heaven was spending the day raking designs in the sand. I asked David what he was thinking about, imagining some sort of soul-searching or meditative enlightenment, or perhaps incipient poetry.

He said, "I was thinking about whether I should pile the leaves beside the road, or on that little berm, or whether I should gather them up and carry them to the compost." One reason he is more content at the market than I is that he can be present in the moment. An admirable skill.

I spend hours at the potting bench or kneeling beside a mountain of soil, moving seedlings and rooted cuttings to containers of fertile soil, potting bare-root plants, and transferring plants whose roots have filled their pots to larger quarters. I take pleasure in working with the plants and appreciate being still enough to tune in to wildlife around me.

Often when I'm working near the big soil pile, a wonderful tinkly song comes from the nearby woods, a sound like swirling of ice in a crystal glass. It's a breath-catching, soul-stirring sound that I finally identified as the song of a winter wren. The wren nests in understory thickets, sometimes running along the ground like a mouse, and sings high in the trees. This welcome songster is said to frequent the jumble of up-turned roots and brush piles—helping me rationalize not cleaning up messy places.

One time I dug soil from deep in the pile of potting mix and came upon some germinated filberts. I sent a thank you to some forgetful squirrel and began potting them. From near where the winter wren sings, a cacophony began and I tried to identify the bird responsible. Soon I realized it was no bird, apologized to the not-so-forgetful squirrel, and deposited a few of the sprouted nuts at the woodland edge.

Another time clucks, loud chattering, and a scrambling sound drew my attention to a nearby young oak tree. I was surprised to see three robins flying just above a fleeing squirrel, their bills close to the back of its neck, as they scolded and chased the squirrel from limb to limb. Both sexes of robin are said to aggressively protect their open-cup nest. Perhaps the third bird was a maiden aunt or mother-in-law. Anyway, I have a notion the squirrel will think twice before approaching that particular nest again.

Often I listen to a jazz-fan bird I've yet to identify, calling *Chick Correa, Chick Correa*. Once I was surprised to hear a red-tail hawk's descending scream nearby. Accustomed to hearing the hawk's cry high in the sky, I wondered what had brought it so near. Looking up, I saw a Steller's jay. I knew jays could imitate other birdcalls, but I'd never before been so thoroughly fooled.

Racing around one mid-April day, in the midst of weeding pots, selecting and grooming plants, I was stopped in my tracks. A veritable symphony was coming from the woods! The warblers were back! The woods fairly burst with their music. I was overjoyed and overwhelmed. I wanted to be able to recognize each of their songs but was a long way from doing so. One struck a memory chord: *wichety wichety wichety*. I ran in the house and grabbed a bird-song identifier Erika had sent, digital-chip-equipped cards that slip into a pocket-sized case for playing. I punched a button. *Wichety wichety wichety*. Eureka! Sure enough, it was a common yellowthroat, a pretty yellow-breasted wood-warbler with a black mask. I promised myself to take a field ornithology class one summer.

In my quest to name the moons, April's should be Returning-Birds Moon.

Along with the return of the birds is the return of the cyclists, large flocks in colors as bright but not nearly so handsome as the birds' breeding plumage, and joggers in sports bras, T-shirts, or no shirts at all, appearing as joyful as the birds at the coming of spring, but lacking the musical celebration.

By the end of April wild iris are blooming lavender, orchid, purple, and blue on woodland edges, beside the road, in upland meadows. Soon deep blue swaths of camas appear in meadows, ditches, and roadsides. Early explorers looked down from hilltops and thought they were seeing lakes below, the camas were so blue and dense. In the spring we are busier than I would prefer, but I get frantic only when I forget to look and listen.

Chapter Eight

The season wound into higher and higher gears. Farmers' markets and track meets pushed into May, when we prepared for more big plant sales at the same time that we tried to maintain our landscape business. May's is the Crazy Busy Moon. Our heads and our lives operated at a frenetic pace, too fast to even consider questioning whether anything might cause us to veer from the prescribed activities on our over-full calendar.

Many of the people we helped enjoyed their gardens coming or going but never really spent time in them. Dorothy was different. She worked side by side with us. Dorothy is a musician, a devout Episcopalian, and at that time was a practitioner of *ki aikido*. These interests were starter dough for hours of conversation. I was particularly fascinated with *ki aikido*. I had taken *aikido* classes years earlier but had learned only the physical movements. Dorothy learned the philosophy. She learned to use *ki*, described as "the real substance of the universe," to strengthen her muscles, her balance, and her responses. She also could "press with *ki*" to send healing energy to unhealthy, sore, or weak body parts. I always looked forward to an afternoon at Dorothy's, wondering what I would learn this time.

On May 11, 1995, we were working at Dorothy's home. She and I began weeding the ubiquitous *Cardamine* (commonly known as little bittercress) and a particularly rapacious bellflower, *Campanula rapunculoides*, digging its deep roots from around the lilac hedge at the back of the property. Meanwhile David did a series of heavier chores. He hauled a ladder out of storage under the garage, hitting his head hard on a beam as he did so. Not apparently worse for wear, he proceeded to grub a cherry stump from the ground with a mattock. Next he used the extension pruner to cut branches high up in the apple tree. Finally he stretched a string along the edge of the lilac bed where Dorothy and I were working and started the edger.

From a distance the edger looks a bit like a toy lawn mower. It consists of a small engine powering a vertical blade and pushed by lawn-mower-like handles. We looked up when we heard the noise of the motor, to assess when we needed to get out of the way. David is always steady and precise with the edger, so I was surprised, watching him coming towards us along the string line, to see him waver. And then he swerved again. I couldn't imagine what was happening. The dandelion digger fell from my hand. As I stared, he stopped the edger, dropped down onto one knee and held his head in both hands.

He gasped, "Oh! My head!" His face was ashen—bloodless.

Dorothy and I rushed to him. I blurted, "Dorothy, would you press him with *ki*?" (A *ki* practitioner can't use *ki* on someone else without being asked.)

She guided him to concentrate on his "one point" and lightly touched his temples with both of her hands. I watched, transfixed, as the color returned to his face. He sat down to rest and, for a while, I went back to my weeding. After a few minutes he said he was going to the truck to lie down. I walked him there and told Dorothy I should get him home. There was a flu going around, and with his headache, and now a woozy stomach, I figured he was getting it.

We'd driven a few blocks when, in a voice combining equal parts confusion and fear, David cried, "What's happening to me?"

Unnerved, I pulled over. "Is what we're doing smart?" I asked him. "Should we be going to the doctor or the hospital instead of home?"

"No, no," he said, "I'll be all right. I just need to go home and lie down."

Foolishly, I listened. We went home and David went right to bed. In the nearly thirty-seven years we had been married, I believe that was the first time he had opted out of dinner. Eventually I joined him, quietly so as not to disturb him. His sleep was fitful; he was in almost constant motion, but through the years he had often been a restless sleeper. I vacillated between worrying about him and wishing he would be still so I could sleep. A particularly intense episode, a kind of rhythmic rocking, accompanied by a warm moisture spreading beneath him, jarred me wide awake.

"He wet the bed!" I thought. "What is going on?"

I leapt out of bed and fumbled through the pages until I found "seizures" in my medical book. Trying not to panic, I decided that first thing in the morning, we would go to the doctor.

At first light, I told David it was time to wake up. We needed to go to the doctor. I knew he would object, but I would insist. But he didn't wake up. Initially this wasn't distressing, as he often slept soundly. I remembered how frustratingly hard it had been to awaken him when our first child was ready to be born and I needed to go to the hospital. So I kept trying.

"Honey, it's time to get up! David, you need to get dressed so we can go to the doctor. Wake up, honey! David?"

I gave him a kiss and a hug and put my hands on his face but he slept on with deep, even, relaxed breaths. He seemed so comfortable. He probably really needed his sleep. But I was determined—although, in retrospect, clueless.

He needed clean clothes, so I decided that if I started dressing him, surely that would wake him. Laboriously, I took off his clothes. David is not a big man but he's definitely bigger than I am, and he was not cooperating. I heated some water and washed him carefully, then worked clean sweat pants around his legs and hips and finally got a shirt over his head, and his arms in the holes. Still he didn't wake.

"Honey, we've got to get to the truck. You need to wake up. You need to walk." I could help him but I couldn't carry him, and I certainly couldn't lift him into the cab of our big F250 Ford pickup. I could barely step high enough to get myself in. At last I realized that I needed help.

The thought floated through my consciousness that we'd promised not to do anything heroic if the other one was seriously ill. "Yeah, sure," I thought. "And let him lie here until he starves to death?"

I didn't want to leave him alone but I had no choice. This was back when most telephone conversations were conducted on landlines, but as we had no electricity we had no phone in the trailer. And I needed to call the doctor. I yanked on some boots and ran the length of our long driveway and down the hill, a distance of about a city block, to the Randolphs, our nearest neighbor. We each live on parcels of at least twenty acres, so homes are not close together on this hillside.

I banged on the doors of the main house and of the mother-in-law mobile. No answer. I banged again. Nothing. I turned and ran back up the hill as fast as I could, dimly aware that the boots had been quick to pull on, but were not a good choice for running.

I ran past our drive to the next property, about a quarter-mile uphill. Here two neighbors live side by side, each on the inside edge of their twenty-acre lot. I dashed to the first door, but again got no response. A ball of fear was rising from deep in my body. I ran next door and knocked again, exhaling in relief to hear footsteps. Jack moved slowly and was having increasing memory problems, but he was right there for me that morning. He led me to the phone. I called our doctor, babbling out my story to her nurse.

In careful measured words the nurse said, "Hang up. Call 911 and tell them just what you have told me." Which, of course, was the logical thing to do, but not the one that had come to mind.

I had a terrible time getting the 911 operator to accept my directions: "Go a half-mile up Easy Acres and look for a driveway on the left. They'll see the nursery sign."

She wanted an address, but we didn't have one, as this wasn't a recognized residence. She thought I was being irrational—hysterical—as I kept explaining how to get there rather than giving a number address. Finally she understood, and I ran back home to check on David. He was still sleeping deeply, seemingly comfortable. At last I allowed myself to think the word "coma."

Soon—ten minutes? fifteen?—I heard a motor and jumped to the window to see the paramedics' red Jeep speeding up the driveway. Four men hurried in and took David's pulse, blood pressure, and other vital signs, which they radioed back to somewhere. I hovered on the back edge of the bed, not wanting to get in their way in the tiny space, but unwilling to be farther away. I was glad our wandering dogs had chosen this morning to wander so I neither had to calm them nor worry they would be underfoot. They always returned eventually.

"What's his age?" a paramedic asked.

"Sixty," I responded, for some reason. In fact, he wouldn't be sixty for another seven months.

They strapped him on a stretcher and noted that it was too wide to maneuver through the trailer's narrow passages to the main door. Twisting the stretcher and balancing carefully, they managed to get him out an unused bedroom door whose steps had been shoved to the side, asking me as they left which hospital they should take him to.

"The nearest," I said, which would be Sacred Heart in Eugene. "I'll come in a few minutes." I wanted to try to get my bearings, think about what I was doing, and not chase right behind the EM Jeep. I ran a brush through my hair, grabbed my purse and, attempting to assemble some inner calm, drove the nearly twenty miles to the hospital parking structure.

Heading for Emergency, I tried to walk briskly but not run, tried to breathe deeply. I checked in, saying, "I'm with David Hess."

The receptionist said, "Oh. You're the girlfriend?"

"I'm the wife." I said.

She looked at me over the top of her glasses. "They told me the girlfriend would be coming." I realized they probably assumed the little trailer was a love nest. Surely no wife would put up with living like that!

But girlfriend or not, they showed me into the inner sanctum. The emergency doctor told me it was probably a brain aneurism, explaining that an aneurism is a weakness and bulging in an artery wall that can break, causing hemorrhage. He said David would probably survive, because "people usually either die in the first few minutes or they make it."

I called our daughter Erika, who said she would cancel her classes at the university, where she was teaching French, and come right over. On the phone she asked, "What's wrong with your voice?" My throat felt almost closed and the fear ball from below my stomach had grown nearly to my mouth. I could barely talk.

Erika and I stood beside the gurney where David lay. We watched the neurosurgeon poke and prod, testing David's reflexes. One poke elicited a grunt and a protective body movement—a lot more than I'd been able to get. We looked across the gurney at each other, sharing the thought that the doctor, a young man, short, stocky—a bit reminiscent of a middle-school line-backer—seemed awfully rough. He gave us a horrible litany of potential outcomes. David could die. Or surgery could kill him. He could have a total personality change. He could lose sexual interest and function or it could become obsessive. He could survive but be a vegetable. Erika and I connected eyes again.

We heard but we didn't hear. We heard the doctor's words but didn't accept their meaning, and hoped David's subconscious wasn't listening. We just stood, watching David. I gazed at the face I had first known on a smooth-skinned, crew-cut eighteen-year-old with hair so short I couldn't tell it was curly. I'd watched the changes of forty-one years: his bushy red beard now with silver side-walls, the once orderly eyebrows sprouting willful hairs curling this way and that, his skin gradually weathering. Now he lay on the gurney, his graying sandy hair curling around his sun-lined face and over his ears. We watched his chest rise and fall. We listened to him breathe.

Six inches of stiff tubing protruded from the top of his head where the emergency doctors had drilled a hole to release the fluid pressure. Hemorrhage can block the ventricles, the four continuous cavities in the brain that allow circulation of the cerebrospinal fluid, thus building pressure that compresses and displaces brain tissue. If this pressure is not relieved, it will cause coma and, ultimately, death. In the next weeks we would become very familiar with the effects of fluid pressure.

Our son Jeff, his wife M.A., and their two children drove up from southern Oregon, where Jeff was teaching school. They left their kids, eight-year-old Celina and ten-year-old Nate, with old friends, Kathy and John Gillespie, for the night. Our friends Hannah and Jake Wilson joined us, and David's mother and brother traveled down from Bremerton. We all sat uneasily in the ICU waiting room for the surgery that could save David's life—if it didn't kill him. The list of possible awful consequences recited pre-surgery had been a ghoulish ritual. Yes, I realize the surgery itself might kill him, cause a stroke, paralyze him for life. But, okay, have at it. I signed my permission.

I'm not sure how we spent the five or six hours of surgery—walking back and forth, making small talk, murmuring to others who were waiting for word of their own loved ones. Having my family and dear friends there helped hold me up. And at the same time I felt that our combined energy would certainly find its way to David. My throat was tight and my heart beat fast.

I tried to turn my thoughts to the busy life we had so suddenly left behind. Who needed to know that we wouldn't be there? We had made plans to bring nursery plants to a big sale the next day. I must call and cancel. And the following weekend would be a UO track meet. Someone else would have to do David's job of coordinating the field communications. I made calls. I paced some more. Our gathered group talked sporadically and softly, but we indulged in no what-ifs.

Around midnight the doctor appeared and began explaining what had transpired. He had peeled back the skin on David's head from the top of his forehead above his right eye to the front of his ear, and cleaned his brain. The whole right hemisphere was filled with blood, and as essential as blood is within the veins and arteries, it is toxic to the cells when it escapes its vessels. The doctor had found and mended one small, still-intact aneurism, but he hadn't found the source of the bleed. A small percentage of cases mend themselves, he told us, but the medical community doesn't know why. I thought of Dorothy's pressing David with *ki*, and remembered the color coming back into his face, and

I believed that in this case, at least, I knew why. But I didn't share what I assumed would be repudiated.

The doctor said David was still in a coma, but gave no indication of how long it might last. I remember his saying something to the effect that David was not yet out of the woods. Our friends went home and Jeff, Erika, and I collapsed on the floor and couches of the ICU waiting room, where I would spend at least one more night.

Eventually we were allowed to go into David's room one or two at a time or, if the right nurse was on duty, sometimes we could sneak in three. In his room a bank of machines and monitors flashed and beeped, numbers blinked, solid or broken lines went up or down. Little suction cups were all over his chest, with cords attached connecting them to the many machines. His head was bandaged, swami-style, with the tube still protruding from the top. He slept, noisily sometimes, at other times deeply and evenly. We talked to him, held his hands, sent him strength and good energy. And he slept on.

David's surgery was on a Friday night. The following Sunday was Mothers Day and when Erika arrived at the hospital she presented me with a big bag of vitamins. I couldn't imagine anything more appropriate for the moment. I'm not sure at what point in her life my daughter and I switched roles. I remember her steadiness, supporting me through my parents' last months when she was twenty-one. Perhaps that was when. And there was the time, a year or so later, when she put an arm around my waist and made me sing, restoring my breathing from a panicky bout of exercise asthma. But from very early in her life she was a nurturer. At her fourth birthday party she seemed to feel so responsible for the pleasure of her guests, furrowing her brow and checking repeatedly on each of them, that she appeared more the first-time hostess of a dinner party for sixteen than a carefree birthday-girl. I once thought she would be a psychologist, watching her seeming to intuit the problems and needs of the neighbor children. She even showed more empathy and consideration for her dolls than I ever did for mine. She made clothes for them and dressed them and gave them elaborate lives. When I was a child I lined my dolls up in a row and informed them they had the privilege of watching me go about my independent play.

Now, a few weeks before her thirty-sixth birthday, our daughter paused her graduate studies and her teaching, brought me a bag bulging with vitamins, and most important, brought herself, totally focused and supportive.

That Sunday morning before Jeff and his family had to get back to their jobs and school, Erika suggested I take advantage of both her and Jeff's being there to go back home and bring the dogs to her house, which was about a mile from the hospital. She went on to urge that I consider sleeping in a bed myself, using her place as base.

It was hard for me to leave, and I buzzed inside with anxiety the entire time I was away, worrying about David and also about the dogs. I had left food for the dogs, and the vet had assured me: "They're predators. They'll be fine." Still, I stewed. But when I started up the driveway there they were, springer Sadie with her long floppy ears and muscular spotty half-Dalmatian Issa. What a relief! They were lonesome and hungry but safe. I ushered them into the truck, grabbed their beds and food, and headed back to town. I dropped them at Erika's and was back at the hospital, having made the round trip in a fretful hour and a half.

Erika and I looked out the window of David's room to the little people scurrying about many floors below. They rushed into stores, across the street, towards campus, towards town. Everyone was in such a hurry. "They think what they're doing is so important," Erika said. It was startlingly incongruous. All these people below so desperately busy, so alive, while here in this room we had put our busyness on hold as we focused on what *we* thought was important—helping pull David back into his life.

That moment has returned to me innumerable times through the years. I think of the apparent tempo of the lives of the people we watched when I feel pressure building in myself. And I think of David lying there and the activities he had recently considered essential. In the midst of a *hurry-worry-tick-tock* moment I ask myself, "So what would happen if I didn't get this done? Would the world still turn? Would water still cycle? Would the birds still nest?" And I remind myself to breathe deeply, relax, hold on to the moment—to live it, to love it.

In a few days David began having brief conscious periods. Some of the earliest times he was agitated. "We've got to get going! We've got to get out of here!"

"Why do we have to get going, David?" I asked him.

"We've got plants to load."

I tried to explain that the plant sale had come and gone without us, days before. But it didn't seem so to him. "We've got to make a plan!"

One time we found David, a long-time smoker, looking frantically around the room and pleading, "There must be some kind of tobacco around here somewhere!" But eventually he became more relaxed—not accepting, because he didn't seem to have any understanding of the situation—but at least no longer agitated.

From day to day and hour to hour, David went in and out of consciousness, but when he was awake he always knew us and was happy to see us. Every time he was awake we were exhilarated. Every time we couldn't reach him or he was confused, our hopes crumbled. One time Jeff's wife came in wearing a blue mask so she wouldn't spread whatever germs were ailing her, and the doctor asked David if he knew who she was.

"Sure," he said with a grin. "That's my blue-nosed daughter-in-law!"

We often explained to him what had happened and where he was. He never seemed particularly concerned and would frequently even make wisecracks. We told him he'd had brain surgery. "Will it make me smarter?" he asked brightly. But the next time we came, he wouldn't remember any of it, or even that we'd been there.

One evening after many hours at his side, Erika and I finally went home—to Erika's house, where I would curl up with the dogs on her couch—and were nearly ready for bed when the phone rang. It was the ICU neuro-nurse, saying that David was asking for us. We whipped on our clothes and dashed back, thoroughly adrenalated, not knowing what to expect.

"Hi!" he said happily, reaching for our hands. "Hi. I just wanted to see you. I was afraid you didn't know where I was."

Sometimes when David was awake, he was very clear-headed. Often we would have good, though brief, conversations about things that had happened years before. We tried to think of ways to stimulate his memory and ways to help him back to the present. Erika and her partner, Bob, made tapes from jazz CDs to play for him on our cassette player, and David reminisced about which musician played with whom, and when and where he had heard them perform. We surrounded him with pictures of family and friends as well as beloved dogs and cats, all of whom he enjoyed identifying and telling stories about. We wished we could bring

Sadie and Issa to visit or at least Mr. Cooper, Erika and Bob's dog, who (unlike our dogs) was very well behaved.

My emotions roller-coastered in parallel to the highs and lows of David's consciousness, but once I began to feel reasonably certain that he would indeed live, financial worries began to seep into my own awareness. I called the insurance company in a bit of a panic and a most reassuring and empathetic woman explained that our 20 percent would be required only until the bill hit $5,000 (long past), and then the insurance would pay 100 percent. I was so relieved I felt faint. Later I began worrying about even that $1,000, not to mention basic living expenses, as I wasn't working and probably wouldn't be for some time. Occasionally when friends asked what they could do to help, a little voice inside me would say, "Just send money!" But I shocked myself even acknowledging the inner voice. I certainly would never have let it out.

I grew up taking care of my own problems, as did my parents and their parents before them. I'm a little island that has chipped off other islands and spawned more islands of my own. "My do it myself!" my younger sister insisted at age two. "I'm my own boy," my three-year-old emphatically declared to my sugary adorations of "my" boy. My pre-teen daughter preferred to open her own door and carry her own bags, thank you very much, not just as a budding feminist but also as one feeling and respecting her own strength and ability. The grandmother I never met froze to death because she chose to find her own way home through a snowstorm after her car got stuck in a snow drift near a neighbor's house.

My friend Hannah knew all of this about me, so she approached the subject tentatively when she told me that she and Jake had written letters to mutual friends, and, through the Episcopal church where we were inactive members, had set up a fund for us.

So what happens to an island when dear friends build a bridge? She weeps. She accepts the traffic. Perhaps she is saved. But she is changed forever. And at some point she begins to realize that she never was really an island at all. Beneath the surface of the water she is interconnected with other apparent islands, with valleys and ridges molded by the water and forces deep within the earth. She is part of an entire mountain chain— everything connected to everything else.

Chapter Nine

One morning mid-way through David's second week in the hospital, we found him sitting up in bed, working a crossword puzzle—or so it seemed. We were ecstatic. When the doctor visited, David reached out his hand with a hearty handshake. The doctor asked him, as he always did, if he knew where he was. For the first time, rather than "No" or "Where am I?" or "McKenzie-Willamette?" (the name of a near-by hospital where I had been a patient a few years earlier), he answered correctly: "Sacred Heart Hospital."

"So," asked Dr. C., "why are you here?"

"I broke my head."

Then the doctor asked him how long he had been in Eugene. David looked apprehensive and gave a quick glance at me as if asking for help. "Well," he said, "Evelyn came in 1955."

The doctor prompted, "And when did you come?"

"She came in 1955 so I came in 1957."

"Good. So, how long have you been here?" asked Dr. C.

David looked confused. The doctor asked, "Do you know what year it is now?"

"It's 1995," David answered, to our delight.

"So, how long have you been here?"

Desperately, David shot another look at me. "I need a piece of paper," he said.

"Okay," said the doctor, handing him pencil and paper.

David wrote down 1957 and then 1995. He looked and looked at them. Erika, Bob, and I watched him, practically holding our breath, willing him to figure it out. He looked some more, doodled a little, and with a flourish announced proudly, "Twelve years."

David's more lucid periods always related to the position of the bag that collected the fluids from his brain. The rigid tube projecting from his head connected to a flexible tube that emptied into a bag hung at varying levels. If the bag was too high, he'd be groggy and confused or asleep. If the bag was low enough, he would seem almost like his old self. I often felt frustrated that they didn't just leave it at the level where David was most alert but, in hindsight, it may have been to avoid draining too much fluid from the brain or, more likely, to monitor more easily whether his ventricles were able to take over the re-circulation on their own. But even when the bag was low and he seemed completely clear-headed, he could rarely remember what had just happened, where he was, or why he was there.

One day he recounted an elaborate delusion. He imagined he was staying at the home of the UO's assistant track coach (which is where our grandchildren had spent David's first night in the hospital—his surgery night). In his mind, the Gillespies had a "sort of hotel," and there were track athletes in the other rooms. He was quite sure he wasn't at the hospital; he was at the Gillespies'. It was such a strong delusion that he remembered it as fact weeks after he finally understood what he had gone through. I wondered if it wasn't evidence of the subconscious mind at work. When he was comatose we had mentioned that the grandchildren were staying with John and Kathy, and once they had visited when he was still sound asleep.

When David was awake his mind was active, sometimes in surprising ways. Once at lunch he asked me to lower the side of the bed so he could sit in the chair. I didn't know if he had permission to do that, but anyway, I didn't know how to drop the side. So he told me! Somehow, while he was lying there hooked up to a half-dozen machines, he'd been able to investigate under the bed to determine which button to push and which bar to slide to let him out of bed.

The next morning we found him in a new room, nearer the nurses' station, where they could keep an eye on him. It seemed that during the night he'd entertained himself by rearranging all the little suction cups on his chest, causing the machines to record very interesting, if not very helpful, data.

Dr. C. kept waiting for the ventricles in David's brain to assume the job of recycling his cerebro-spinal fluids, but they seemed incapable. I began to feel responsible. If only I had realized what was happening sooner. If only I had acknowledged that I needed help. If only I had brought him right in. I was working myself into a trembling, hyperventilating state of guilt.

Initially I had been put off by Dr. C.'s blunt manner, but by this point, I revered him. To me he was not just a masterful surgeon; he was almost a magician. At last, I sobbed out my guilty fears, asking him if David's system would be responding better if his care hadn't been delayed. Dr. C. spun around, looked me straight in the eyes, and unhesitatingly unburdened me. No. It made no difference. Time sometimes is a life or death matter, but he didn't die. And there's nothing else the overnight delay would have done. Whew! Thank you, Dr. C.!

When David had spent about three weeks in the intensive care unit, the doctor decided not to wait any longer for his ventricles to function. If he was to retain consciousness and regain brain function, it was essential to avoid excessive intracranial pressure. If the ventricles weren't going to kick in, and we didn't want him to continue forever attached to tubes and bags, another surgery would be necessary. The doctor would install a permanent shunt to pipe fluids from David's brain into his gut, freeing him from his exterior plumbing.

After the shunt was installed, David was moved out of ICU and began what Dr. C. estimated would be a couple of years of mending to get to whatever level of recovery he was capable of attaining. At his first attempt to stand, his brain didn't seem to give him an accurate picture of his body's position in space. He stood awkwardly, bent at about a 45 degree angle. With effort and direction from the therapists, he found the vertical and took a few steps. As he gained strength I began taking him for walks on the hallway loop around the nurses' station. He had a belt harness I would hold onto to keep him from falling down, although I wondered if I'd be strong enough to do more than break his fall. We joked about taking him for a walk on his leash.

Along with other strength and balance exercises, the therapist had David walk on a thick mattress. Erika and I chuckled in uncomfortable concern as he tipped and stumbled, and the therapist said, "You try it." So we took off our shoes and tried to walk on what felt like a springy, spongy mass of ball-bearings. David was getting a good work-out. We didn't chuckle again.

Now that the tube was removed from his head, we decided to do something about his lop-sided hairdo. The left side of his head sported a rumple of longish sandy-blond curls. The right side had been shaved. Erika asked the nurses if they had any barbering tools. All they could come up with was some tiny manicure scissors, but Erika wasn't deterred. Soon the left side of his hair was militarily short and tidy, almost a match for the right. He sat there with his fuzzy graying red beard and his short hair, smiling. He liked the effect. To this day when it's time for a hair cut, David asks if I can cut it short "like Erika did in the hospital."

David's spirits were amazingly good. He didn't seem frightened or frustrated or the least depressed. He would plunge confidently into every new challenge and not seem particularly concerned about its difficulty. The brain-function information the hospital gave us was that "the right-hemisphere-injured patient may be less aware of his disability. He may be oblivious to even the most obvious inability or feel he can return to normal activity immediately." This contrasts with left-hemisphere damage, which leaves the sufferer all too aware of the problems, and prone to anxiety and depression. The same reference notes, "The hypothalmus controls appetite, sexual arousal, and thirst. Injury to this ... area brings on mood swings [and] inappropriate behavior, and deters motivation to work toward independent goals." In the past several weeks I had learned more about the brain than I would ever have known to ask. Now I wondered what our future would bring.

One evening Erika and I stayed late at the hospital while David was watching television. When a commercial showing a big, juicy cheeseburger came on, he immediately wanted one. He *really* wanted one and he wanted it right away. We checked with the nurses but the kitchen was closed, so Erika called Bob, who put the writing of his doctoral dissertation aside and headed for the nearby Burger King. Bob, a strict vegetarian, hadn't been near a fast-food burger place for probably twenty years. Besides that, his Jewish upbringing declared cheeseburgers non-kosher, as they combine meat and dairy. Nevertheless, Bob soon arrived with steaming cheeseburger in hand, filling the room with its fleshy fragrance. David ate it happily and seemed to see nothing extraordinary in having his slightest wish granted at midnight in the hospital.

As David's condition improved I shifted my focus from trying to be with him nearly every waking moment to preparing for his homecoming. The first essential was a cell phone. Never again did I want to go running from neighbor to neighbor in an emergency. I brought one home expectantly and tried it from the trailer. "NO SERVICE," the phone screen fairly shouted at me. I tried it on the south side of the hill. Still nothing. I drove up and down our road, trying it at various locations, and then for a mile or so each way on the highway below, but could get no reception. Back to the store.

They suggested a bag phone: a more powerful, bigger, heavier phone that, appropriately, you carry in a bag. But that didn't work either. Finally, adding annoyance to my frustration, I found out that a competing phone company had a tower within my range and the folks I'd been talking to simply hadn't wanted to tell me about it. A cell phone from the company owning this closer tower worked only from the south side of our property, but it did work, to my immense relief.

As David's rehab sessions became more intense and it appeared his release was imminent, I began worrying that someone at the hospital would assess our rudimentary living situation and determine that I couldn't take him home. The possibility of rehab at a nursing home had already been mentioned, and that was with the assumption that we were living like normal people. Might the paramedics have mentioned that the ground was rough, the stairs unstable, that we were without electricity or plumbing? I could imagine a Medical Grand Master proclaiming, "No patient shall be released to a sub-standard dwelling." I've always had a horror of nursing homes, and anything short of our own home seemed to me to be giving up, or giving in to dependence. Certainly it would signal the end of the life we were living and intended to continue living. I never wanted either of us to have to leave our simple life in the woods.

I needn't have worried, but it still took a while to quell my anxiety. In retrospect I think the nursing home was suggested as an option if there were no one at home who felt comfortable in the supportive role. After the original suggestion it wasn't mentioned again, possibly because of our very negative reaction. And no Grand Master ever asked if we could pass the Acceptable Conventional Life-style Test.

After being released from ICU, David seemed to be on the express schedule out of the hospital. Before another week had passed, less than a month from his arrival at Emergency, he was released and we accepted Erika's invitation to stay with her for a few days. David was almost giddy with joy. He'd been wanting to "get out of there" since his first brief awakenings. Now at last he could get on with his life. The dogs wagged and licked and tried to jump on him. The four of us took over the room of a thoughtful housemate who went to stay with a friend, giving us our own space and preserving Erika and Bob's privacy.

Erika and I took David to our favorite acupuncturist, his first such experience. He accepted the needles with his customary equanimity and came out both more relaxed and more energized. Patti, the acupuncturist, said David seemed like someone who had looked over the edge and decided, "No, I'm not ready to go there yet." I was grateful he'd had the chance to "look over the edge and decide," although he remembers no decision. Since his hemorrhage I've heard of many folks who didn't have that chance, whose cerebral or aortic blood vessel broke and they were gone. No chance to look over the edge, or look back, ready or not.

On his second day out of the hospital David wanted to go to the track meet. Jeff had come back up from southern Oregon and he, Erika, David, and I all trooped over the three blocks from Erika and Bob's house to the field. A friend I'd not seen in a while greeted me, but looked wide-eyed at David, with a sharp in-take of breath. I didn't understand her reaction. Compared to where he'd been, I thought he looked great. Certainly he was paler; his hair was only beginning to grow out where it had been shaved; perhaps his scar showed; maybe his eyes were a bit starey. But he looked wonderful, albeit a bit fragile, to me.

After about ten minutes in the stands, he got antsy. He didn't want just to watch. He wanted to work. His thought processes weren't nearly clear enough yet, and I couldn't imagine he'd be physically strong enough to climb the steps of the grandstand to the press box. But off he strode, with Jeff not far behind him.

I was glad and comforted that Jeff was there. He had always been a helpful and caring person. I remember him rescuing a two-year-old maiden-in-distress when he was not yet four, and getting in trouble in grade school for helping slower students after he'd finished his own work. (His teacher wanted him to stay in his seat.) Now a teacher and coach, he supported his students and athletes in ways that would fortify their spirits as well as their minds and bodies. And as one active in track—coaching, officiating, and competing—it was appropriate that he should accompany David.

Jeff ran to catch up with David and lend him an arm if he needed it. David stopped to visit along the way and to rest numerous times as he climbed up the long grandstand steps. His colleagues welcomed him back but a friend told him months later that he only needed one look to know he could not put David to work. It was all right, though. He was happy just to be there.

We stayed at Erika's for a week before we packed up our dogs and headed back to our woods. On the way home we stopped at a shopping center to get supplies and we went into the store together. David soon got tired and said he would wait in the truck. He stepped confidently away and turned—in the wrong direction. I stopped in the middle of paying the clerk, my heart thumping wildly, to watch through the window. Finally I saw him turn back toward the truck.

Typical, I think, of many architects, David had always had an unerring sense of direction. I do not, and had always counted on him to get us wherever we were going. So it was distressing to me to realize he no longer had that sense. I was going to have to be the grownup, and I was going to have to learn fast.

As we continued home the dogs snuggled happily in the cab of the truck, Sadie between us, Issa on David's lap. When we turned off the highway, they lifted their noses and began making little whinging noises. They stood up and looked ahead, wriggling and panting in excitement. I breathed deeply for the first time in a month—or so it seemed. "Hi, woods!" one of us said. And "Whew! We made it!" It seemed as if this moment had been the goal since that morning of May 12, when I realized David was not going to wake up. Here he was—awake, upright, and beside me. And we were back in our woods, on our own. We turned to each other and clung in a long tight embrace.

Chapter Ten

David got stronger in the sunshine. We took gradually longer walks up the road, with me holding his hand, not his leash. I was anxious and felt protective but he remained mellow and optimistic. Eventually, I relaxed a bit.

By the end of June, he decided he was strong enough to return to selling plants at the Farmers' Market, which we had then been doing for seven or eight years. The market had never been a major source of income—that mostly came from the landscape business—but we appreciated the three to four thousand dollars it brought in during a season. And at that point we had no income from any source. So partly to add a few shekels to the pot and partly because David was eager to get back into the world, we decided to test his readiness. First we'd load and unload together and I'd hang around for most of the day, gradually staying less, and finally leaving him to do it alone. He was happy to be at the market again, and glad to see old friends. I was delighted he was strong enough to rejoin the world, and at the same time, fretfully thinking of work to be done at home, I was doubly gratified at his independence.

David had smoked since he was thirteen, sneaking behind the barn with his friend Paul. The army fixed the habit deeply in his psyche and physiology. As he matured and became more health conscious, and particularly after being harassed by his wife and children, he tried to quit—several times— but it never took. After two weeks in the ICU, the nurses told us that all vestiges of nicotine were out of his system. Now the challenge was just psychological. A number of market vendors as well as customers were smokers and David told me he was frequently tempted to have just one, because it would feel so good—but he knew that one would inevitably lead to more. He was proud of resisting the urge and enjoyed telling friends who were trying to quit that it was easy. All they had to do was have a cerebral hemorrhage and spend a month in the hospital.

Late in July, Erika and Bob got married and then moved to Mississippi, where Bob, a brand-new Ph.D., had accepted a job teaching Latin American studies. They were married on the velvet carpet of a manicured croquet court at a bed and breakfast run by some of our friends. I volunteered us to build a rustic *chupah* from filbert and oak branches. Historically, that sort of project would have been simple for David, and I would have been his assistant and go-fer. His cheerful demeanor convinced me that this day would be no different, so I started bringing branches. He looked hesitant. He held the branches, shuffling them this way and that. I suggested we begin by making an arch and he said he wasn't sure how. I gulped, completely unprepared for that response. When he tried to bend the pieces in the reverse direction to what was necessary, I realized I had made a big mistake getting him into the project. He seemed mostly oblivious to the challenge, but I sensed an underlying unease in him. Maybe it was my own. Together we muddled through and, after an afternoon's frustrating work, made a hobbit shelter that the bride and groom stood in front of, rather than under. At least no one laughed at it. I felt awful, though, having put him through that, but he didn't seem at all distressed.

Some months later when we visited Erika and Bob in Mississippi, the lesson came home again. Erika had asked David to design a simple hanging basket for a staghorn fern that she wanted to hang in a tree. He accepted the assignment confidently, asking for pencil and paper. He held the pencil, looked at the paper, and after some time drew a lopsided triangle. That was all—and that was with great mental effort.

Erika and I met eyes over his head. The doctor had said it would take up to two years to mend the severed nerves and regain whatever abilities would be restored. David had doodled, designed, planned, and drawn all the years I had known him. Husband and father had been returned to us but it appeared it would be a long time, if ever, before the return of the architect.

Back home, David continued to gain strength in body and in mind. We held hands when we walked because it felt good, rather than for encouragement and support. I worried less about leaving him home alone as long as he had the cell phone. I went back to doing gardening jobs for the clients who had been patient enough to wait for me, and jobs I particularly enjoyed.

Summer's long days began to shorten and the calendar said it was fall. In my mind that time is all a foggy blend. I did what I needed to do, pretty much on automatic pilot. But abruptly in mid-autumn there was an almost audible "pop," like ears unplugging from a change in altitude. Six months had passed since David's hemorrhage and I suddenly reawakened to the world around me. Leaves were turning clear yellow, amber, and caramel. Birds chattered in the rose bushes and a cool breeze played with the loose hair around my face. The last time I had noticed, the leaves were baby green and the birds were singing songs of love. I kicked piles of leaves and inhaled the musty fragrance of fall. I wanted to shout, "Hello! I'm awake!" The odd thing is that I hadn't known I had been asleep.

Some years earlier, when I was in a deep funk over an unpleasant job situation, I was chagrined to realize that I had completely missed spring. Awakening this time and remembering the earlier experience showed me that I had within my grasp therapy far more powerful than pills and far cheaper than counseling. I had been so focused on my pain, my fear, my anxiety, that I hadn't been present in the world. But if I just turned my concentration outward, tuned in to the natural world, I could pull out of myself and come back to life. The birds still sing, the leaf buds unfurl, the earth keeps spinning whether I am sick or well, attentive or ignorant. It's my choice whether or not to come along for the ride. *So old dog*, I thought, *here's a new trick to be learned.*

Sometime that fall I stopped in to visit friends of mine who worked at Hendricks Park, a forest park and rhododendron garden in Eugene. Michael Robert, then the head gardener, told me that a position was open and he wondered if I might like to apply.

"Do you realize I'm about to have my sixtieth birthday?" I asked him.

I don't think he had but, after a pause, he said it didn't matter. The city had a strict policy against hiring discrimination, including age as well as gender and ethnicity.

I had not thought of going back to work for someone else, but it was an intriguing possibility. It would provide reliable, regular income, which we sorely needed. It would include insurance, which had been taking a huge bite out of my meager wages and our plant sales. And it would add to the pension fund I had begun when I worked for the university. Besides that, Hendricks Park was one of my favorite urban places, with oak-shadow traceries playing across emerald green lawns, twenty-foot rhododendrons blooming from February to October, woodpeckers and squirrels busy in the trees. Excitement mixed with trepidation (Could I deal with being an employee again? Could I keep up with the "kids"?) and I applied for the job.

I began gardening at Hendricks Park at the beginning of December 1995, a few days before my birthday. Our day began at 7:00 and ended at 3:30, so I still had a little time for private jobs. I was one of three full-time staff. We were supplemented irregularly by work-study students, youth corps, young people doing prescribed community service, at-risk or alternative-education kids, and volunteers. All of my natural *machisma* came to the fore as I tried to keep up with Ginny, a bright and dynamic young woman just a few years older than our daughter. In her eighth year at the park, Ginny could work circles around most of the men, all of whom were one to several decades younger than I.

Getting used to a new job and routine is always difficult, at least for me. With my poor sense of direction I frequently wondered if I was lost on the park's network of paths. For the first couple of weeks, I was plagued by dreams of incompetence in which I would forget things, lose things, not understand directions, not know how to perform jobs. But before long I learned my way around and loved being in the park and part of an exceptional team.

As the third member of the crew, one of my duties was to do "chores," the euphemistic name for cleaning bathrooms and picking up litter left by visitors the previous day. I alternated between getting obsessive—picking so much tissue, so many plastic bags and candy wrappers from the ground or out of plants that I began to jump at white flowers, thinking they were litter—and being thoroughly disgusted with my fellow hominids, muttering to myself as I picked up bottles, cigarette butts, take-out containers, tampons, and condoms. You often see the slogan, "Your mother doesn't work here. Pick up after yourself." But my mother, at least, would never have picked up after us. We were to put things where they belonged, and inspired by our parents, had far too much respect for the earth (or fear of our parents' reaction?) to ever, *ever* litter.

Michael and Ginny showed me more efficient gardening methods, necessary with a small staff caring for a thirteen-acre garden in a seventy-six-acre park—quicker, less meticulous techniques than I had been using in residential gardens. Ginny demonstrated what she called "guerrilla gardening": more ecological approaches not yet accepted by city management. The official protocol was still to rake leaves out of beds and replace them with bark. Ginny knew that leaves and twigs would decompose in the beds, giving far richer compost, not to mention looking more natural, than bark. So in out-of-the-way areas, leaves from the lawn would go in the beds. And when no one was looking, she would toss fallen branches back under the trees, eventually to become part of the forest duff, rather than piling them up to be carried off site. She was also a devotee of native plants, and together we collected seeds and germinated natives to introduce to the garden.

Going to work at 7:00 a.m. meant that for several months I drove in the dark, frequently on icy roads, and at other times drove to work partially blinded by the rising sun or by the setting sun on the way home. Had I planned on being a commuter, it would have been smarter to live on the east side of town. But I have always believed in living near my work and hadn't intended to commute. Now I was discovering there were practical as well as earth-friendly reasons to limit excessive driving.

I saw many wrecked cars on my way to town, and had a near miss myself. Lorane Highway snakes from Territorial Highway, near our property, into Eugene. As I drove a particularly wiggly stretch one morning, an oncoming car crossed the center line into my lane. At first I thought it was an ill-timed attempt to pass. I uttered a few expletives and swerved to the shoulder. He clipped the driver's edge of my front bumper, which woke him up and spun him out of the path of the car following me. If he had completely missed me on his sleepy trip home from the night shift, he would have hit the car behind me head-on. As it was, the three of us stopped beside the road, shakily exchanged names and phone numbers, and continued on our respective journeys.

But there were rewards in my early-morning travels as well. As commutes go, I had a lovely one. Early on a November morning a wide crescent moon hung in the clouds. Spencer Butte silhouetted black against the pea-green pre-dawn sky, with thin blue-black clouds streaking across it horizontally. In spring curving road-banks were thick with trilliums and false Solomon's seal; dense patches of fawn lilies, with their jaunty up-turned petals and mottled leaves, covered a hillside, and across the road, camas lilies painted a meadow startling blue. Going home in the fall, red, orange, and gold vine maple leaves shone in the evening sun. I arrived at work stimulated and arrived home relaxed, from the beauty of the countryside.

On David's first-year exam, Dr. C gave him a glowing report. We had felt things were going well, but neurosurgeons apparently get accustomed to troublesome if not tragic results. The doctor was thrilled, which made us feel not only happy, but very fortunate.

One weekend evening not long after his doctor appointment, David was late coming home. It had been only six months or so since the doctor had given the okay for him to drive again, and he'd just recently begun to drive solo. Now it was dark and he was alone and it was very late. I paced and watched the clock and imagined. It got later and later and still no David. We had only the one vehicle, so I couldn't go looking. I called voice mail but there was no message. I wondered whether the old truck had broken down. Had he had an accident? Another hemorrhage? A heart attack? I paced more. Called voice mail again. Looked up the road and listened for motors.

Finally I could hear the distinctive rattle and growl of our Ford pickup and relief flooded over me. I flew out the door and ran to meet him. He stumbled out of the truck and stood swaying slightly back and forth, a sheepish smile on his face.

I gaped in disbelief. "You're drunk!" My anxiety turned to rage. I was out of my head angry.

David said, "I ran into Andy and ..."

I interrupted. "How could you? You're barely getting your life back! You nearly died! What were you thinking? You *weren't* thinking!"

"I'm okay," he barely whispered.

"You're *not* okay! You drove seventeen miles at night, pie-eyed drunk!"

He looked shocked and assaulted by my eruption. He took a step back as if from the force of my fury.

"If drinking is so important to you, you can go to Washington and live with your brother and drink yourself silly," I exploded. "I don't want to watch you kill yourself or run over somebody else. I don't want to be anywhere near."

He reached out toward me, but I turned away and walked to the trailer.

The next day when he was sober and I was somewhat calmed down—although still seething and incredulous—we talked. He understood that I wasn't hysterical about the fact of his drinking. If he wanted a beer or two at home that was his business. Even if he wanted to get drunk at home it was his choice. A dumb choice, as far as I was concerned, and not one I enjoyed, but his choice nonetheless. Driving drunk was a far different matter. He heard me, understood, and agreed. After a while it occurred to me that my many times driving cradled in the tight embrace of Morpheus, surviving only by great good luck or a guardian angel, was just as dangerous and irresponsible as David's driving under the influence of Bacchus.

I also understood, for the first time, that David had no awareness of having had a near-death experience. His near death had been *my* experience, not his. He had almost no memory from the moment of the head pain in Dorothy's garden until after the shunt was installed. There were only glimpses of memories, floating images of a visitor or two. And he retains one abiding regret: On the day of David's surgery, Jeff had arranged for his AP English class to visit with Ken Kesey at Kesey's Pleasant Hill farm. Years later, David has not come to peace with the fact that his emergency took away that opportunity. But beyond that, his memories were minimal. He requested and accepted our stories, explanations, and recollections, but had little personal knowledge of any of it, making it understandable, I suppose, that he had no particular feeling of having been saved.

Later he told me that the main thing he learned from his hemorrhage was not to fear death. If things had been different—if Dorothy hadn't pressed him with *ki*, if he hadn't gotten to the hospital on time, if any of the surgeries had not gone well—he just wouldn't be here and he wouldn't have known the difference.

The main thing I learned was that life is precarious and brief; and all the more precious on that account.

Spring 1997, my second year at the park and nearly two years after his hemorrhage, David continued to improve. To most people, he appeared completely recovered. He had stayed resolute with no nicotine and was able to work longer and harder than before his collapse, although he still needed extra sleep. We celebrated the equinox that year with the birth of a granddaughter. At nearly thirty-eight, Erika's pregnancy was not exactly a slam-dunk, so welcoming her first-born was a particularly exciting event.

When Tasha was two weeks old we flew to Oxford, Mississippi, to meet her. Seeing this babe in her mother's arms—my daughter holding her daughter—I had the surprising thought, "I can die happy now."

With no immediate plans for death, I don't know where that came from, but I was filled with an overwhelming joy that Erika would know the pleasure I had known having my children. I floated back to Oregon, my head in the ethers.

After working there a year and a half, it seemed Hendricks Park was an extension of my own garden. Instead of getting lost on its meandering trails, I knew each path and bed, what was about to bloom, what needed moving, where plants should be added. I was deeply attached not only to the park, but also to Michael and Ginny. They had become family.

That second summer, parks crews changed to a schedule of ten-hour days, four days a week. I would work a couple hours at my few remaining private jobs after our 4:30 quitting time, plus all day on Fridays. One of my favorite private gardens was close to the park, a place where I had once wished to be a full-time gardener. A hilltop double lot with a wooded side yard, an old established Japanese hillside garden, and a new flower garden David and I had installed near the front entrance, it was a joy to work in. On weekends I did my inadequate best to catch up at the nursery.

In the early years of our gardening service, when Erika and I had more work than we could keep up with but couldn't afford to hire help, we would laugh that maybe we could convince people to pay *us* to let them garden on our crew as therapy. In a very real way, I found gardening to serve that role. Fingers deep in the soil or holding pruners to shape a plant, watching seedlings or newly rooted cuttings grow and thrive, admiring the effect of a new plant composition—all can relax tight, nervous muscles, erase anxieties, and energize the soul. That fact, along with stubbornness and determination, got me through the summer. But by summer's end, I was exhausted and I felt like my body was falling apart. My back ached; my joints throbbed; my feet could scarcely bear my weight.

At about that same time, the voters passed a tax-limiting measure that would cut deeply into the city's budget. As I was a recent hire, we all assumed I would be cut. I began to research other jobs, along with retirement options. I was sixty-one, and would be eligible for Social Security on my next birthday. When I realized that my small pension, along with David's and my Social Security, would approximate my current take-home pay, my weariness overcame my reluctance to leave and I decided that even if my job didn't get cut, I would retire at the end of the year.

Michael and Ginny threw a farewell party for me. I imagine that after his twenty and her ten years on the job dealing with rules and red tape and bureaucracy, their emotions at retirement time would have been less mixed than mine. But I had been spared the administrative rigamarole; I felt tightly connected to the park and its people. Too tired for emotional control, the tear dams broke. After I thanked everyone for the party, I headed home as a park employee no more.

In the house I sank into one of our two chairs—both hard white plastic. If sinking was my goal, I needed to find a more receptive spot. Heading for the bedroom I grabbed "the pig"—a grayish-pink, stuffed back-support with arms. I tossed it on the head of the bed, pushing it against the closet. As I leaned back on the pig with a sigh, I could sink successfully at last. Tiredness ran down my arms and legs and out my fingers and toes. I was home from the park. What now?

Whatever it was, I could wait a day or two to face it.

Chapter Eleven

I hacked my way to the greenhouse with a machete. Blackberries tore at my clothes and flesh. Thistles scratched and poked. I battled a twisting, grabbing explosion of golden hops, rougher than a cat's tongue, blocking the greenhouse door.

Beware the Jabberwock, my son!/ The jaws that bite, the claws that catch!/ Beware the Jubjub bird, and shun/ The frumious Bandersnatch!

Lewis Carroll's verse swirled in my head as I snicker-snacked my vorpal blade, amputating brambles.

As spring approached on my first year home from the park, weeds overgrew the pots and invasive plants caroused at will. Herb Robert, a delicate-looking European geranium that I had weeded out of gardens and brought here to compost—and apparently also brought unwittingly as seeds on my shoes and tires from Hendricks Park—had long ago escaped from the compost pile and multiplied many times over from transported seeds. Even worse was the *Lamiastrum,* an exotic, boldly variegated, romping member of the mint family. We had been given the *Lamiastrum* by friends (always look a gift plant in the roots!) and thought we'd like it because its pretty silvery leaves would brighten dark places. Herb Robert and *Lamiastrum* both have definite desires for hegemony. Travelling at a kudzu-like speed, *Lamiastrum* has blanketed thousands of square feet and herb Robert borders every circulation route, then marches steadily into the woods. Exotic blackberries were here when we came, although the former owner had grazed horses, which brought a modicum of control to the brambles. With no grazing, the blackberries have increased several-fold under our watch. The thistles were here too, but our tilling and moving of soil has multiplied them.

I pulled and dug, cut, scraped, and hacked, and finally came into the house filthy, bleeding, weary, and dispirited.

"A bit dense out there?" David asked.

"Nothing that a bulldozer and a dose of Agent Orange wouldn't cure," I growled.

After officially retiring (meaning that I accepted a pension and Social Security) I gave up most of my private gardening jobs both to cut down on driving and to have more time at home to maintain the property. Now I could concentrate on the nursery. Now I could weed and organize. But I was staggered by the chaos that greeted me. I had spent weekends the past two years trying to keep up with the nursery plants—propagating, potting, watering, weeding. But I had ignored the grounds. What I faced gave no clues that anyone living there had ever pulled a weed or cracked a horticulture magazine. *Twenty-one acres*, I thought. *Twenty-one acres of thistles, exotic blackberries, and other invasive plants—a mess for every microclimate! I know better!* I howled inwardly.

If I had wanted to rationalize away my frustration, I could have found material. I had attended conferences where the first several hours were spent on definitions. What is a native plant? Native to where? Native since when? How do you define an invasive plant? Should all exotics be *verboten*? Occasionally consensus was unreachable but usually people agreed that, to be considered native, a plant must have grown in a particular ecosystem before European settlement. Even granting that, however, contradictions and questions abounded. North America has experienced both cold and warm cycles that necessarily are accompanied by changes in plant communities. And Native Americans probably moved plants important to them, as they traveled from place to place. Besides that, as the wind blows, the rivers flow, and birds fly, plant parts and seeds will travel as well. So clearly, landscapes aren't static and a new plant is not inevitably a dangerous invader. But I have criteria of my own for whether to declare an exotic unwelcome. It has to behave itself. If it spreads rapidly and crowds out what was there before, I want it evicted.

However, although that seems unarguable to me, it is not to everyone. Once when I was weeding with Ginny at Hendricks Park, a visitor called us plant Nazis. Having grown up when real Nazis were butchering people and infesting nations across Europe, I was shocked and upset by the label. But recently I came upon a writer who took great pains to ally restorationists with xenophobes and fascists. He equates the desire to protect native plants from being overrun by exotics with Hitler's goal of genetic purity and preservation of the homeland. He feels that invasion biology focuses on exotics as threats and intruders rather than on factors that lead to the invasion. He writes of "anti-exotic hysteria," and refers to battling invasives as genocide. If I found his argument persuasive, I would have had a good excuse to ignore the mess that confronted me. Unfortunately for my peace of mind, his rhetoric seemed as extreme to me as he found that of the nativists. So I still had work to do.

I came here excited, idealistic, sophomoric. I had many years of gardening, schooling in horticulture and landscape architecture, respect for ecology, a life-time love of nature—I thought I knew what I was doing. Some years earlier, I had managed greenhouses for a now-defunct wholesale florist, with the help of a young, dedicated, over-educated crew of eighteen. I'd say, "These plants are too crowded" or "We need cuttings from these plants," and the next time I looked, it was done. At some unconscious level, I think I was expecting the same results on our property. But here I'd note that the blackberries were coming back with a vengeance or that the herb Robert was invading the fenced area where we keep shade plants, and the next week they would be worse. The first four years spent trying to spread ourselves between nursery and garden service followed by two years of my being away almost full time had taken a bitter toll. I couldn't accept that reality didn't match the pictures in my head.

I'm not sure what I expected. That David would jump out of a phone booth with super powers, after having already completed his own projects? During our early years here he had spent a good deal of time designing, something I would never interrupt. And he could always find blackberries to cut on the far end of the property, an honorable occupation wherever it is carried out. For the past few years I just wanted him to concentrate on getting as well as possible. So no, I really didn't expect him to be the rescuing superhero.

Perhaps I was looking for the angels, archangels, and all the heavenly hosts to come down and lend a hand? Or expecting that if I could just work harder, work smarter, I could do the work of three or four? Or maybe, as a propagation pro, I could figure out how to clone myself?

I had friends a decade younger who were moving to town because their country place was too much work. But I would not consider giving up. I loved our woods and hills. I was sure I could find a way to manage. I decided that for the time being I would worry less about the jobs to be done, and spend more time studying the world around me. I knew there were still lessons the land could teach us, and I was determined to learn them.

I had always considered myself a student of nature, but it turned out I was a very young student—a kindergartener. It was as if I had spent more than sixty years in a philosophy class admiring the beauty of the teacher, the elegance of her dress, and the wonder of her delivery while being oblivious to her lessons. I'd had a lifelong schoolgirl crush, a reverence; I'd been worshiping from a distance, like one on a sightseeing bus, oohing and ahhhing at the scenery, or at a zoo, laughing at the monkeys in the cage. But separated by glass of windows or bars on cages, I had remained on the outside.

I'd enjoyed hikes, long runs, and bicycle rides through beautiful country, but I was still in, not of, nature. After more than a decade of living on our land I felt more "of" nature, as a member of her family. But as with any family, I couldn't pretend completely to understand the other members or their complex relationships.

Someone said, "The study of ecosystems isn't rocket science: it's much more complex than rocket science." It became clear to me that rather than looking to horticultural precepts, it was important to examine the principles of ecology when gardening, especially in the country. Most conventional gardening has to do with subduing and controlling nature. In order to maintain control one needs superior troops, a boundless bankroll, first-rate fire power, and a clear sense of personal, national, or species supremacy. David and I had neither the troops nor the funds to hire them. We had already decided against the firepower and we didn't want dominion. We wanted a relationship. We needed to learn how to work in harmony with Nature's systems and enlist her aid in our pursuits.

So I began my studies in earnest. Wandering in the hills beyond our property, I noted that wilder areas looked far healthier than places more traveled. Exotic blackberries and Scots broom grew near roads and paths, or where trees had been cut or heavy equipment had compacted the soil. Deeper in the woods, in less disturbed areas, few or no exotic plants grew. The more neglected, the more beautiful. Yet with neglect a lovely garden becomes a weedy mess. So question number one was: What's going on? And how could I apply whatever it was to my own property?

The next thing that stood out, in my quest for deeper understanding, was the diversity of plants. In wilder areas I found no monocultures. Ground covers wove a tapestry. Low Oregon grape and foamflower poked through carpets of evergreen violet and ginger. Twinflower mixed with snow queen, vanilla leaf, and wild strawberry, all in a bed of moss with tiger lilies or iris, trilliums, fawn lilies, or fairy bells emerging through it. The combinations shifted and re-combined, adding, subtracting but always dense and diverse. Also furnishing the forest floor were decaying logs, stumps, and tree branches, themselves covered with moss, lichens, and a variety of higher plants. Above the floor, plants grew in multi-layers: snowberries and salal, tall Oregon grape and baldhip roses, red huckleberry and oceanspray, red flowering currant, vine maple, and dogwood. Higher still were big-leaf maples, white oaks, and Douglas firs, each layer less varied than the one below but still a mixture of species and ages.

My third take-home observation was the dense layer of litter beneath all of the plants—dead grass, fallen leaves, twigs, fir needles, torn-up bits of fir cone, cast feathers, animal scat. The top layer was coarse and easy to identify. Below that the duff began to break down and component parts were possible but difficult to distinguish. Lower still it became well decomposed, a dark, rich humus. This lesson was apparent. The natural mulch insulates the soil and moderates its climate. Not so obvious was the fact that many of the groundcover plants germinate in the mulch, their roots barely reaching the soil. Less obvious still was the underground world that breaks down the litter, releasing nutrients for the plants and combating soil diseases and plant-eating arthropods. An important adjunct to this particular lesson was the fact that no one put a rototiller or shovel in the ground. Seeds or pieces of plant dropped into the moss or forest litter. Fertilizer came from the microorganisms or fell from the trees. And no one—at least few humans—walked among the plants, squishing the oxygen from the soil with their boot soles, evicting critical soil life.

I could easily see how to apply lessons two and three—plant diversity and a thick layer of mulch. Lesson number one was more of a conundrum. The lush healthy plant communities were in undisturbed areas, but a garden is by its nature a disturbance. Invasive plants cluster near paths and roadways, but my garden is where I live. I must necessarily walk and occasionally drive there. Perhaps part of the lesson was that I would never win the battle against the invasives, in which case I should concentrate on keeping them from the wilder areas and not beat myself up with less than perfect results near the road. Another part of the lesson was to find any way possible to decrease the disturbance, particularly by honoring the soil as a critical strand in the web of life. Another may be a re-play of the old belief that if you save someone's life you are responsible for that person forever. As I make a garden, I interfere with natural succession, allowing some species to prosper at the expense of others. In order to stop the natural progression of plants—annuals to perennials to shrubs to trees—I must continue to maintain it.

As I planned a way to put these lessons to work, I continued to observe the natural world and read everything I could get my hands on about gardening in concert with natural systems rather than by trying to control them. I benefited particularly from *Weedless Gardening* by Lee Reich, a soil and plant researcher for Cornell University and the USDA (although I think we grow weeds better than east-coasters do!) and from permaculturist Toby Hemenway's *Gaia's Garden*. Finally, with summer already begun, there was the perfect opportunity for an experiment. We were late in planting a vegetable garden. We had not gardened during the recent over-programmed years, leaving the only sunny flat land available to be overtaken by grass, snowberry, blackberry, and an assortment of herbaceous weeds. No time to dig or till. Let's cross our fingers, we decided, and take the plunge.

We mowed the area as short as possible, grubbed out numerous woody plants, and watered well. We dusted chicken manure on ground intended for beds and carpeted the area with thick sections of weed-smothering newspaper, carefully overlapping them like shingles on a roof. Next we soaked the newspapers, topping the planting beds with several inches of compost, and covering the paths with wood chips. Tremulously (how could this possibly work?) we planted seeds and transplants into the beds, often pushing a knife through the paper where roots—we hoped—would eventually travel.

Then we held our breath and waited. Astonishingly, we were blessed with a luxuriant, almost weedless garden: tomatoes, corn, squash, beans, salad greens the first year; we added strawberries, raspberries, a winter garden, and a small orchard the following year, all with a minimum of weeding and, except for raspberries, asparagus, and fruit trees, no digging.

We mulched the beds, using Nature's top-down approach, and in successive years we would just pull whatever weeds had drifted in and add more compost, poking seeds and plants into the thick organic layer. Without digging or tilling, we avoided bringing buried weed seeds to the light, to germinate in a happy explosion. We learned that the oxygen added to cultivated soil stimulates furious microorganism activity, adding nutrients to the soil but using up organic matter, necessitating the addition of fertilizer to maintain health. No digging and good compost from the top shades out weeds and encourages microorganism activity—and therefore fertility—at a steady rate.

I was thrilled with the garden's success and with the idea that I might have the secret for doing more with less work. Of course I still had to find time to extend the new method to each developed area, and I'd still not learned how to clone myself. But at least I had reason to hope. And I sincerely welcomed Nature as my gardening ally.

I have learned and changed, living in the woods, but sometimes I feel that rather than learning, I'm re-learning, hovering on the edge of ancient memory. Once I must have known not to build my hut on the low ground, known that if I burned the trees I would kill the fungus that feeds the squirrels, known how the light and the song birds tell what plants are ready for harvest. For my own health and safety I must have known to watch and listen to the species around me and to understand how we all affect one another. If a genie gave me three wishes, one would be that, for the health of the human species and our Earth home, we could again learn that ancient wisdom.

PART THREE

Fifteen Summers

Chapter Twelve

While baby green new growth is still soft on the fir boughs and the solstice is a fortnight away, summer can arrive abruptly and with great wildness. A few days of rain and a couple weeks of humid warmth: bingo—we're living in a jungle. The grass is head-high. The mailbox disappears and I can't find the paths. I search for the sickle, but my blood races, exulting in the wild fecundity. The increased tempo and crescendo of song from the trees tell me the birds concur.

One near-summer day I was cutting grass and weeds and stacking seed-starter trays behind the trailer. When I came back around the corner, a big doe was munching happily on plants I had set out for the market. I suggested she graze elsewhere and she bounded into the tangle that had once been our display garden. Then I saw her tiny spotted fawn *inside* the compound protecting potted nursery plants, an area enclosed by six-foot-high chicken-wire fencing. Incredulous that it could get in, I wondered how to get it out. I opened the gate but of course that frightened the fawn farther inside. It ran to the far end of the compound and started crashing into the woven wire, scattering pots this way and that. Mama doe was on the other side of the fence, dashing crazily back and forth. I had intended to scoot beyond the fawn to herd it back to the gate, but as it flipped pots and threw itself against the fence, I knew the solution had to be quicker than that. Moving as quietly as possible and talking softly to the terrified babe, I scooped it up. I remembered childhood stories (myths, but I didn't know that) of mother animals abandoning babies who had the smell of humans on them, and was glad I was wearing gloves. The fawn screamed—more of a bleat, really. The doe wheeled frantically from side to side, eyes wide and wild. I lifted the fawn over the fence, mashing down the chicken wire, but not enough to get close to the ground. As the fawn leapt down, I said to the doe, "Here's your baby, Mama. She's okay."

When the fawn jumped from my hands, it doubtless felt as if it were escaping, rather than that it had been rescued. Later mom and babe were at the end of the drive and the doe watched me over her shoulder for a long time. If this had been a Disney film, we would have heard the strumming of harp strings and the doe would have batted her long lashes, whispering,

"Thank you!" But I think it far more likely the long look meant, "Don't even think about coming near my precious child ever again!"

The doe had munched a few of the market plants, but I'd interrupted her before she did too much damage. Later, we discovered short-term protection for plants left outside the fence. We had heard that *zoo-doo*, manure from big cats, was an effective deterrent to deer browsing, so we wondered how they would react to territory marking by humans. Following the lead of dogs and other creatures we've watched, David and our visiting son-in-law set out to pee an invisible fence. I"m not sure what David thought, but Bob got quite a kick out of it. A fence like that might be a challenge to maintain, but for a brief period it worked beautifully.

In mid-June I gasp to see the showy orange honeysuckle in full bloom, looping through filbert, oceanspray, and sarvisberry. Poison oak is blooming too, loose grape-like clusters of tiny yellow stars with orange centers. I try to keep it away from paths where those more sensitive than I might touch it, but I enjoy watching flickers eat its berries later in the summer, and seeing its fiery red foliage before summer's end.

Pink checkermallow opens, along with delicate sky-blue flax and blue-purple wild onion. Oceanspray is in full, fluffy bloom by mid-summer. Its foamy inflorescences of tiny white-to-cream flowers give it its name, though *oceanfoam* might be more appropriate. I love this shrub. It's a wildlife garden in one plant. Several butterflies use it as a host plant (meaning—*gasp!*—butterfly larvae eat the leaves) and numerous birds use it for shelter, forage for insects along the stems, and eat the persistent brown seeds in the winter. Another early-summer beauty is the red elderberry, which is beloved by birds. Voluptuous pyramidal clusters of scarlet berries quickly disappear before a flock of cedar waxwings or thrushes.

If I still get to name the moons, I'll call June's the Fecund Moon.

One day I saw another fruit eater, a western tanager, its shocking red head, yellow body, and black wings flashing, as it dove, spun, and appeared almost to fall, catching insects in the air. Apparently tanagers frequently dine on insects, but usually pick them from branches and leaves of shrubs. It was sometime later that I watched cedar waxwings fly-catching over the pond, much more gracefully than the tanager. I knew that fruit- and seed-eating birds often fed insects to their young and maybe that's what the tanager was doing. But it was late in the season when I watched the waxwings, and their hatchlings would already have fledged. They had to be eating the insects themselves. Later I was serenaded by a winter wren from the woods nearby. I have always felt his song to be a special gift, and I breathed a quiet, "Thank you."

In the summer of 1994 I heard a car in the drive and was thrilled to find my three oldest nephews. Jim, the middle of the three, had designed our pond, so I took them down to have a look. We caught up on their lives a bit as we walked to and from the pond and then I was chagrined to realize I couldn't take the next decent step. I couldn't ask them in or offer them a place to stay for the night. With some awkwardness I brought out drinks and we visited in the driveway, but I felt disappointed, frustrated, rude.

Through the years I tried to ignore my inability to be welcoming and my nearly constant annoyance at not having a way to organize and retrieve things in our little shack of a trailer. But in June of 2000, after seven and a half years living there, I had a major meltdown. I had been looking to this as the date when we would have the mortgage paid off on our house in town and would therefore be able to get another loan to start work toward building a house on our property—a house that would allow us actually to invite people in. All this time I'd been putting up with the trailer by spending the bulk of my time outside and by ignoring my surroundings when I needed to go in. But I had mentally focused on June 2000 as the magic moment when our trajectory would shift toward our new house. When the mortgage bill came, I examined it for a change.

What's this? How could we still owe so much? The balance should be near zero by now. David, who was as mellow in the trailer as a monk in his cloister, said no, the balance was correct. We still had a year to go, after all.

I couldn't believe it. How could I have been so confused? When I finally realized how wrong I was, I dissolved. Everything I'd tried to ignore came pushing its way past everything else: The trailer was turning to compost. It wouldn't last another year. And even if it did, I couldn't. Couldn't tolerate another winter in this drafty, dirty, uninsulated hovel. Couldn't abide the damp, the mold, the rust. Elastic waistbands and nylon stockings rotting and sagging; my high-school-graduation portable Olympia typewriter's keys frozen with rust; wind-up clocks winding down until they died, their mechanism oxidized; zippers failing, clothes stinking, and boxed envelopes pre-glued.

How could I submit to another year of the disarray of clothes in piles, of winter mud and summer dust, of the smell of mice? Another year of not having even a clean surface to write on, let alone a room of my own? Another year of not having anywhere to *put* anything? Another year of having to remove piles from the lids of storage boxes or from in front of a drawer in order to put anything in or get it out? Another year of not being able to walk across the floor without *bumping into* someone or something?

In those famous studies of rats going cannibalistic in crowded spaces, I'll bet the females were the first to turn. I wonder if they devoured their mates first, or their children?

Two things snapped me out of my self-pity, waking me like a splash of cold water in the morning. The first was a radio interview. Everyone old enough to remember the Vietnam War can recall the heart-rending images of a Vietnamese girl, napalmed clothes aflame, running to the temple. The interviewer asked this now-mature woman if she was bitter. Oh no, she said. She was happy. She felt very lucky. She felt love. She had met a wonderful man. They had fallen in love, married, and now had a cherished son. She was completely happy and felt forever blessed. The interviewer asked if she still had pain from the burn scars covering her body.

"Oh yes," she answered gently.

"How do you tolerate it?" the interviewer asked.

"I just don't focus on it," she said. "When the pain is too great, I go outside. I look at the flowers and listen to the birds and I'm grateful."

The other thing that turned me around was an article in *National Wildlife* magazine describing the ecological footprint of an above-average Indian family. Jyoti Khandelwal's family lives in Delhi, India, in a five-room house. She shares the five-hundred-square-foot space with her parents and ten other relatives—that's about thirty-eight and a half square feet per person. Our trailer is nearly three hundred square feet for just two people. I looked around at our piles of clothes (Jyoti and her family probably have a couple of changes of clothes each) and our mountains of books, magazines, reports, first drafts, ads, letters, and junk mail. I wondered how many acres of trees it took to make all this paper—and it wasn't even from fast-growing trees like poplar, or better yet, from hemp.

E. O. Wilson says it would take four more planet Earths for everyone to live like the average American. And that's just to house the humans. If everyone lived as Jyoti does—a substantial step up for many—our one Earth could sustain us all.

I was chagrined at being so shallow, so selfish. I am incredibly lucky to live in the midst of this natural beauty; doubly fortunate to have my husband healthy and beside me; and blessed beyond belief to live in peace and good health in a part of the country young enough not to be completely exploited and tamed.

In June 2001 we paid off our mortgage and, shortly thereafter, took out a new loan. In September 2001 we submitted our land-use application. The following February it was accepted. More permits and inspections would be necessary; the trailer floor continued to warp and slump, and the cracks got wider, necessitating ever-larger wads of newspaper and rags. I wedged them in; the cat scratched them out; I tried again.

We went on to survive several additional winters in the trailer and I rarely forgot how lucky I was. When something annoyed me, I tried to translate my complaints into plans for our new house: I wanted it to be sound and insulated and to have plenty of natural light. I wanted to be able to organize and store things and keep things clean. I wanted space to work and to visit with small groups of family or friends. I wanted to catch rainwater, re-circulate gray-water, and to be powered by the sun. David noted my requests and assigned them to his mental design program for the day he was ready to design again, which possibility he never doubted. He added no requests of his own. On rare occasions he too had seemed a bit stressed by the congestion in the trailer, the narrow spaces that allowed only one-way traffic. But generally he acquiesced. The trailer was what it was. We were where we were. When the time was right we would do something else but, for the time being, we would be just fine.

I was not always equally serene. But on those occasions when dreaming wasn't enough and I did feel overwhelmed, after grumbling or cursing or heaving a deep sigh, I had only to go outside, listen to the birds, and watch the tree boughs ruffling in the wind to regain my equilibrium.

One mid-summer morning as I was eating breakfast, two sleek, buff-colored largish birds, bigger than robins but smaller than crows, spread their tail feathers and plopped side by side on the top of a fence post. The post looked too small for the two of them, but they didn't seem to mind being crowded. They nuzzled each other with their bills and murmured softly, staying long enough for me to run for my bird book. Their size and short necks, along with their small heads on round bodies, were diagnostic of doves but I wanted to confirm the species. It took more than one book to find a mention of the intense pink legs and feet I was seeing, but sure enough, these were mourning doves.

Mourning doves are typically as devoted as these two seemed. They not only are monogamous but often remain so from season to season. When it's breeding time, the male gathers twigs, rootlets, and other plant fibers and brings them to his mate, whose job it is to build the nest. She apparently is more interested in snuggling and whispering sweet nothings than she is in house building, from the looks of the platform-nest she builds. My bird-guru, Dan, says that, from beneath, you can often look up through holes in the loose and simple construction. I wondered if the eggs might fall through, but obviously it is rare that they do, or the species would be in decline. On the contrary, in spite of tens of millions of mourning doves killed each year by hunters, the species is estimated in the hundreds of millions. Clearly, an elegant nest is not required for success.

I watched the pair of doves admiringly, thinking (anthropomorphically) that they seemed no less loving and happy for having such a humble nest. The next time I heard their hollow owl-like sounds during the day when no owl would be calling, I smiled with the memory of the ardent couple on our fence post, and gave David a big kiss.

I had another glimpse of feathered devotion in mid-July on a field ornithology trip. A female pileated woodpecker blasted out of the woods into the opening before us, *wuck wuck wucking* as she flew. She swooped to the top of a high metal power pole and began drumming. She would drum and then cock her head to listen, and then drum again. Dan said she was probably calling her mate. She stayed there for a long time, drumming and listening, drumming and listening. I still wonder if something happened to the mate or if eventually they found each other. Pileated woodpeckers are another species that form long-time pair bonds.

Throughout the early summer, birds are nesting and bird babies are hatching. One July day I was walking with our daughter and granddaughter, Erika and Tasha, when we realized that the ground just ahead of our feet was moving. Many—probably upwards of twenty—fuzzy, inch-long, tan and black-marked quail babies were crossing the path, from one protective shrubby area to another. I could hardly believe we hadn't stepped on any. We froze. They froze. We carefully backed away and the stragglers followed their siblings to the safety of the undergrowth.

Another experience with a ground-nesting bird didn't turn out so well. We had cut a grassy area and were distressed to discover the mower had exposed a nest with six or eight perfect eggs. I fretted and hoped the parent would return to warm the eggs. The next day I saw that she had indeed returned to her unprotected nest—a pile of feathers was strewn about nearby. Several days passed before some predator came for the eggs. It was a sad way to learn not to mow—or prune—during nesting season.

July 2004 found me sleeping in the dog pen beneath a Douglas fir, its branches spreading wide like a mother bird protecting her brood. I was sleeping outside because Lupi, our granddog, who was with us while her family was in Costa Rica, was afraid to come into the house with Caesar the cat. We were in the dog pen to be sure Lupi didn't stray. She gave me a good excuse to sleep outside, which was my preference anyway. I believe I will proclaim July's moon to be Outside-Sleeping Moon.

The stars were shiny specks salted about the dark bowl over my head. When I was a child I loved a story about a fairy named Poppy. In one picture Poppy stood inside an upside-down colander, the light shining through the holes. The night sky reminded me of Poppy's colander. I understand early people's stories as they tried to comprehend the shape of their world.

In the distance a screech owl warbled his haunting tremolo once, twice, six times and then, in a vibrato a fifth higher, his mate answered him as I drifted off to sleep. Waking in the moonless night I saw the tree twigs blending together to become shrouded branches, a watercolor rendered in shades of black. It made me wonder how to evaluate what I see. Could I trust my eyes if I were called as a witness? Wouldn't the light make a difference? Or my mood or my preconceptions or my memory?

Early in the morning a Swainson's thrush swirled his lilting song up and up, urging the day to begin. Obediently, the sun began to push above the horizon and paint the firs russet and bronze. Bird silhouettes darted across orange-pink clouds and other birds flew into the tree above me, gleaning breakfast from the twigs. A solitary crow cruised and called and soon was joined in flight and conversation. Sun rays reached above the knees of conifers to the east and south of my lair, turning them green-gold. Cloud puffs floated white against robin's-egg blue.

"Get up! Get up! It's a new day! There's work to be done. Mouths to feed!" called a cacophony of birds, or so it seemed to me, still lying warm in my sack. In the early light my guardian fir re-incarnated from a blurred watercolor back to its coniferous state, needles clearly silhouetted against the morning sky. Lupi lay still, her eyes on me. She didn't stir until I did.

Lupi and I are hunter-gatherers. As we hiked up the hill, she wove a circuitous route sniffing, chasing, pouncing; I scrambled up banks and down into ditches, foraging on sweet dewberries and blackcaps. I dashed delighted to a lone thimbleberry, exulting in beating the animals for a change. Lupi's nose lifted in the air or dipped to the ground as she ran, excited. I got a thrill beyond the pleasure of eating as I explored, perhaps some deep genetic memory akin to what motivates Lupi. But I feared we were both too domesticated to fare well if we were abandoned to the wilderness. She didn't seem to have a predator's instinct to kill, I thought. She might accidentally kill something—a quail baby, perhaps, squished by her pouncing paws—but if she did, would she know what to do with it? And if she happened to swallow that tiny ball of fluff, she would get about as much nutrition as I did from my coveted thimbleberry.

As Lupi got more accustomed to the wilds of western Oregon—so different from her Flagstaff home—she became a more efficient hunter and I decided that she might indeed be able to survive on her own. I'm not so fast a learner. I would love to have the skill, the vision, the knowledge of the First People who roamed these hills. Lewis and Clark would certainly have starved if not tutored and served by people tuned in for tens of thousand years to the Earth that sustained them. The early explorers surely would have died, and so would I have.

As the season progressed, my gathering instincts shifted from looking for things to pop into my mouth to searching out seeds and starts for the nursery. I noted the blossoms and calculated when their seeds would be ready for harvest. First I watched for ripe trillium and fawn-lily seeds, next camas, tiger lily, wild iris, orange honeysuckle, dogwood, and red-stemmed ceanothus. The lilies, along with columbine, delphinium, and buttercup, are best planted fresh. Berries like dogwood and honeysuckle need their flesh removed and their seed well washed, followed by a cold treatment to stimulate germination.

And what might I collect as cuttings? Mid-July is the beginning of cutting season. I'm always on the look-out for particularly nice colors in red-flowered currant, which are reliably reproducible only vegetatively.

Seeds—as is the case not only with plants, but with all of us who reproduce sexually—contain a mixture of genes, getting DNA from both parents, so no particular color or other characteristic can be guaranteed. Ninebark and red-stemmed dogwood are easy from cuttings, and most willows will root even if you don't want them to. Vine maple and oceanspray are better from seed.

Lupi continued hunting, sniffing, pouncing. If I took too long searching for seeds and cuttings she would disappear, but come running back with my call. Eventually we would return from the hills and get to work. Happy and exhausted at the end of the day, we curled once again under our protective Douglas fir.

Sometime later David and I agreed to care for our son's dog while he was out of town, and spent the night at his house—my first under a roof for months—to avoid an extra trip between the evening and morning feeding. I woke and felt almost panicky. I was sleeping in a shoe box! The lid seemed to press down toward me. The walls were close and solid except for two small holes for light and air to squeeze through like toothpaste through its tube. The bed was comfortable but the ceiling was only about a third as high as the lowest limb of my guardian tree. I looked up to the starless shoe-box lid. The walls pushed in toward me. I usually filled my lungs with fresh night air, but that night I quelled a mild hysteria that I might have nothing to breathe at all. I heard the hum of the neighbor's heat pump and the purr of cars on the street instead of the mellow calls of owls. I needed to be reminded why a house is a desirable goal. At least at night. At least in the summer. At least in the Pacific Northwest.

One summer we turned our backs on the trailer and set up camp by the pond. David bought a tent, which initially disappointed me: I like to sleep under the stars. But the tent had a fine mesh roof that let me look out while giving him the enclosure he preferred. At night I'd breathe in the sweet air and fill my head with the night sounds: haunting baritone hums and moans of the bull-frogs, excited yips of coyotes, repetitive toots of a pygmy owl, deep *hoo huhoo hoo hoo* of the great-horned owl.

Near the tent we made a table of a piece of plywood over saw-horses, covering the table with a pink and green plaid plastic tablecloth. On this we put the camp stove, along with a stack of plastic shelving to hold herbal tea, yogurt, cartons of muesli and rice, dish soap, and a scrubby. Beneath and beside the table were enclosed boxes for plates, flatware, and kettles, olive and canola oil, tamari, salt, and peanut butter; and a cooler stocked with ice. Five paces or so to the other side of the tent, the solar shower—a five-gallon plastic bag of water, black on its back to collect warmth from the sun, and equipped with attached hose and nozzle—hung from a fir branch. The rungs of a step ladder leaning against the tree provided shelves for soap, shampoo, David's razor, towels, and wash cloths. A mirror fit snugly between the top of the ladder and the highest step. David hung a three-foot plastic pipe from another of the fir's branches, and this became our closet rod. A clothesline between willows on the far side of the kitchen held wet towels and dish cloths.

We luxuriated under our shower, watching birds doing somersaults in the air above the pond as we bathed. The chance to move about without bumping into each other was a more-than-welcome change. We ate looking out over pond water the color of French-onion soup. Overwhelmed with our riches, I felt as if we were vacationing at an exotic resort.

David bought a thin, hard cutting board designed by a skateboarder whose parents considered him a disappointing goof-off. The young man imagined a cutting board made of skateboard material. Tight and non-porous, it would minimize absorption of flavors or bacteria. He made a million dollars and went back to skating.

Just down the hill from the pond lay our garden; it took only a quick dash to harvest fruit for breakfast or gather dinner's corn or salad greens, tomatoes, or carrots, but it was a bit of a trudge back up. For one of our favorite dinners I grabbed garlic from our shed, ran down to the garden for basil and arugula, and pulled out the skater's cutting board. I smashed and minced the garlic and chopped the greens fine. Added just enough salt and olive oil plus some chopped nuts, and *presto* (in about half an hour) *pesto!* Slow cooking at its slowest, but gratifying.

One morning, following my usual routine, I put on the teakettle and scooted down the hill to pick fruit for my morning yogurt and muesli. Trying to decide between strawberries and raspberries (or should I pick blackberries growing just outside the garden fence?) I got sidetracked pulling weeds. Finally I decided on a mixture of all three kinds of berries and filled my container with their fragrant beauty. Returning to the campsite, I was aware that another advantage to living outside was that, when I forget the teakettle, I needn't worry about burning the house down.

Chapter Thirteen

As much as I love summer nights, in the daytime the plants and I begin to sizzle starting around mid-July. When I used to water the research plants at the university greenhouse, I would grumble about the antiquated technology and I swore never to drag hoses once I had my own business. Like so many pronouncements I have made, that one turned out to be a bit ironic. Compared to our initial method of pumping water into gallon jugs, I consider the gravity-fed hoses we now have to be state-of-the-art. And spending most of my summer hours moving slowly among the plants holding the end of the hose, I not only see what's going on with them (Who is about to bloom? Who needs fertilizing or weeding? Who needs a bigger pot?) but also get a front-row seat for watching the wildlife.

A song sparrow whistles and trills from a fence post, *Twee twee tweedle-tweeeeee-tootle tootle*; a spotted towhee, showy with his black hood, white belly, red sides and, the source of his name, spotted wings and tail, sits on top of the chicken-wire fence, his bright red eyes trained on me as I, in turn, watch him; a streak of shimmering indigo precedes a Steller's jay's raucous *shaaaar*, his cacophonous squawk proving once again that beauty need not speak in a soft voice. I get to see baby garter snakes wiggle to their hiding places, chipmunks peeking out from theirs, and on rare occasions, a rubber boa, a smooth brown snake I'd seen only wrapped around the arm of an adoring four-year-old at a nursery-school before we moved to our woods.

One day I laughed out loud to see a sparrow perched on the edge of a water-filled garbage can suddenly jump into the water, flutter back to the edge, flitter and fluff his feathers, and jump back into the water again. He repeated this routine a dozen times or more. Perhaps he was just performing his morning ablutions, but he appeared to be having a rollicking good time.

Between mid-July and early August my woodland mornings become abruptly quiet, so that moon can be the Quiet Bird Moon. From late spring the avian chorale announced the coming of the day each morning and bade it farewell by dusk. But now, it is as if the disc jockey went out for coffee and forgot to cue up the next CD. Presumably the babies have fledged and whole families may be packing their bags in preparation for their long trip south. Warblers, tanagers, and hummingbirds prepare to fly, four- to seven-inch birds traveling as far as Central America and beyond.

The birds know that air and water have no borders. What happens in one country profoundly affects the health of another, or the species who journey or dwell in either. Scientists found traces of Mt. St. Helens' ash around the world within three days of its eruption. Dust from Chernobyl quickly appeared throughout the northern hemisphere. Air I breathe may have been in the lungs of Desmond Tutu or George W. Bush. Air and water are shared by all.

I was distressed when an environmental group I support called for the protection of our dwindling wild places by limiting immigration. This seems to me startlingly short sighted. While we pollute air and water in other countries, while we pump oil from their ground and cut trees from their jungles, while we patent seeds that have grown for centuries in the soils of other lands, how can we refuse their people admittance? Overpopulation is indeed a problem, and the U.S. population is increasing mainly by immigration, not by birth. But it's neither moral nor possible for the U.S. to close its borders so that our citizens can continue to live in paradise with no worry for the hellish state of the rest of the world. Unfortunately, we here in Eden are using up the world's resources, not just our own.

Thich Nhat Hanh says that humans are on this earth to overcome our illusions of separateness. Perhaps we need the birds with their dual citizenship to remind the rest of us that Nature's gifts and processes can't be subdivided into discrete cubicles and parceled out among nations or corporations, each cubicle with its resident bird, pedaling an exercycle to get the work-out formerly found by flying through a neighboring bird's airspace.

Our nursery gets pond water but our neighbor's sole water source is our shared well. From late summer, when the bears might be inclined to make sprinklers of our water lines (though we first blamed that on raccoons), through the winter, when we worry that pipes might freeze, we haul our domestic water in five-gallon containers from a valve outside the neighbor's house. But from late spring and through most of the summer, we leave the valve at the top of the long pipe from their house to ours turned on. Then we can have access to the well water from a valve at the bottom of the pipe, nearer to our living area.

For the first several summers, as the heat increased, it seemed that some problem would always arise with our shared supply. Finally we two households invested in a two-thousand-gallon holding tank, which we thought would put an end to fluctuations. That was shortly before the dramatic visit of the bear family. But once we fixed our perforated line and had Emerald Water deliver another two thousand gallons from their big tank truck, our problems seemed to be solved.

Then one hot summer day when our neighbors, Ruth and Dennis, were out of town, we got a call from their house sitter. Patricia was having trouble with the water. Her instructions had been to turn off our valve if her pressure got low because we had drained the lines more than once—thanks to raccoons, bears, and occasional carelessness. But even after turning off our supply, she still couldn't obtain a good flow. She would turn the water off to let the well re-charge, then turn it back on. But before she could finish washing the dishes, it would go off again. Her guests were going without showers, and flushed the toilet infrequently enough that someone commented on the smell. She said the guests were good sports and had joked that when they went back to California they'd have stories to tell. But Patricia was worried about Ruth and Dennis' garden. So David and I pumped about two hundred gallons from the pond into our truck-tank, drove up the hill, and watered the garden. For our domestic water supply, I went to town to fill five-gallon plastic containers that had built-in faucets. We laid those containers on the kitchen counter, turned the handle, and *voila*! running water at last.

A couple of days later we checked Ruth and Dennis' garden again, and found the plants badly wilted. This time we pumped three hundred gallons and headed back up the hill. Their drive is steep and the truck stalled under our heavy load. David swore, stabbed the brakes, and shifted into first. The truck jerked and the tank flew out the back of the pickup, flipping over and sliding down the drive on its open intake.

I wanted to cry watching the precious water pouring out but, with over a ton of water weight, there was nothing to be done until it was empty. We did manage to shove it enough that the water ran in the ditch instead of down the road.

The force of the fall had knocked the ball valve out of the outlet where we attach a hose, breaking off one of the handles we use to open and close the valve, and stripping some threads. David tried to re-connect it as we got increasingly anxious. Without the valve we couldn't use the tank. We couldn't afford a new tank, but without one our own plants would die, as would the neighbors' garden. Finally, gingerly, even with the damaged threads, he made it fit. So we pumped more water into the tank, watered the garden, and pumped another three hundred gallons for ourselves.

By the time I started my watering it was getting late and I prayed for good pressure so I could finish before it was time to fix dinner. But I got a very limp stream. With good pressure I could empty the tank in seventy-five minutes, but at this rate, it would take nearly three hours. I tried to get extra air out of the line, "burping" it at the tank valve and at the valve into the pot yard, but that didn't improve anything. Disconnecting the hose from the tank, I felt for clogs. Inside the hose was something hard and round, something that felt a bit like the ball in a valve; eventually I discovered the mystery ball-shaped clog was a snail, its hard shell almost completely filling the hose. Trying to get at it with my fingers, I succeeded only in pushing it farther into the hose. In the end, I found needle-nosed pliers with narrow enough pincers to grab the snail and pull it out.

I managed to get the most desperate plants watered, and finished the rest the following day. A couple of weeks later, after they had returned home to an insecure water supply, we got a call from Dennis. He and Ruth were having a cup of coffee on their deck when they heard a dripping sound from under the kitchen. It turned out the water line to their refrigerator's ice maker had become disconnected. Once it was re-coupled, both of our households had well water again. Our big storage tank greatly decreases our anxiety, but having an idea of the many things that can go amiss, we have learned to appreciate, but be vigilant.

One mid-August day heat rose from the ground and blasted down from above, with the two forces meeting on my baking body. The resin of fir needles and the cooking-jam smell of hot berry bushes perfumed the air. I watered until I felt dizzy, while the thermometer pegged at one hundred degrees Fahrenheit. Our granddogs, Homer and Ruby, emerged from under the trailer where they had been hiding from the sun and looked at me as if to say, "You don't expect us to put up with this, do you?" David and I were caring for Jeff's dogs while Jeff's house was being remodeled. They loved our property but were accustomed to the protection of a home in extreme weather. Over-heated and exhausted, the three of us made our way slowly down to the pond. Like a couple of water buffalo, the out-of-shape old city dogs buried themselves in the mud at the pond's edge, only their noses and the tops of their heads exposed. This out-of-shape old country woman sat nearby on the pond bank in the shadow of a Douglas fir. All of us were still as possible, sucking in the shaded air.

This heat wave had been deadly, killing several people in California as well as in eastern and midwestern states. Victims were usually older and living in trailers or other modest uninsulated homes. The media warned people not to go outside and there were calls across the country to provide air conditioning for the needy.

The dogs and I sat in the shade of the trees and I thought of the people approximately my age who lived in dwellings similar to ours. I wouldn't consider spending time in the trailer on a day like this, but I had an option: I had shade. I thought it odd that there was such a fuss about air conditioning while no one mentioned planting trees. Granted, a newly planted tree would not shade a person immediately, but the sun will shine tomorrow as well. Trees outside of buildings, pocket parks in housing developments, and street trees not only cut the sun and cool the air as they transpire water, they also metabolize carbon dioxide, decreasing a cause of climate change. Air conditioners are expensive and use energy, thereby increasing the problem.

While I was pondering all this, the dogs continued their water-buffalo imitation. I lay back on the pond bank watching the dragonflies, and savored the faintest of breezes as it ruffled the leaves above me.

Dragonflies and damselflies, according to the books, are indicators of the diversity and health of aquatic ecosystems. I appreciate them for their prodigious ability to devour mosquitoes, as well as for their beauty. As I watched them, I was awed by their variety, their intense colors, their diaphanous wings with intricate veination, and their fantastic flying. They dart about, fly forward and backward, ascend as much as a hundred feet, spiral around and, flying in tandem, mate in the air. Some are black with bold white spots, some intense reds and blues, some large with blue bodies and iridescent green heads. Some hover like hummingbirds. Some perch high on thin blades of grass.

Watching the dragonflies, I became aware they were feeding on a swarm of ghost-like insects, so thin—with so little substance—I could barely see them, although they were probably a good half-inch long. The back of their bodies curled up and bore more sharply up-curved tails. I hoped that would be diagnostic when I went to look them up. The amazing thing about them was that they were bouncing crazily above the water surface. It was as if they were on thousands of invisible trampolines, or perhaps each was attached to a tiny unseen bungee, jumping, jumping, jumping. They would fly to the pond in a cloud and then, as if on cue from the hand of a hidden conductor, begin bouncing a couple of feet above the pond surface. Occasionally the dance would briefly break and they would swirl upward, just to return again to the incessant bouncing.

Eventually I discovered these were Mayflies, from the order *Ephemeroptera*. Most of their lives are spent as aquatic juveniles but as adults, true to their Latin name, they are indeed ephemeral. They emerge to their adult form with no mouths, no feeding mechanism of any kind. They live from a few hours to, at most, a day or two, with reproduction their sole assignment. The strange bouncing was mentioned in the literature but not explained. I have to assume they somehow were fertilizing eggs and dropping them in the water to begin new lives and provide more food for the dragonflies.

Driving to and from our hills, we watch the grass turn from green to tan as our rainless summer progresses, watch it being mowed, admire the cut rows like ripples in beach sand. By mid-summer in a good year haying machines have returned to their sheds and hay bales and rounds have been trucked off to market. The valley is in its clipped-poodle phase—acres of tightly trimmed gold stubble interrupted by fluffs of green trees and shrubs along ditches and streams, on mounds, on hills.

At home the earth is cracking. The same clay that swells when wet, making the pond bottom tight, shrinks on the surrounding desiccated ground, leaving jagged cracks an inch or more wide. When I look down into the cracks, I can't see a bottom. I drop a pebble and listen. No thud as it hits soil; no clink as it hits rock; no plunk as it hits water. No sound at all, not even the Chinese version of "Hey! Knock it off up there!" Perhaps it is falling still.

August can have Cracking Earth Moon. Or because it was in August that the bear stole the garden fertilizer, and again in August when David, Lupi, and I stood face-to-face with the bear who wanted Lupi's food, a fitting name would be Hungry Bear Moon.

A hallmark of summer evenings is the songs of crickets. They sing most intensely in the warmest part of the summer, and are most active in open grassy areas. The relatively narrow grassy spot around the trailer produces a proportionally narrow and focused cricket chorus, but on the south side of the hill where we hope one day to build, warm weather brings them out in full voice.

Late one hot summer day I sat on a log looking out at the wider sky beyond our house site, the evening full of crickets. Innumerable ensembles in a variety of pitches, cadences, and tempos hit my ears, filled my head and my entire body. I envisioned primitive dancers gyrating around a fire, drums beating, dancers spinning, faster and faster until enveloped in a great sexual ecstasy. As I was nearly ready to burst with the sound, a screech owl's mellifluous warble from the woods behind me tingled my senses. My breath quickened. My mind shattered. It was like some sort of joyful insanity. In retrospect, after my mind rejoined my body and my heart slowed down, I wondered at the power of a little night music. What brain receptors might have been stimulated? What chemicals might have been produced?

As a child I had frequent migraine headaches. In the midst of a headache I would sometimes have nightmares in which I would hear repetitive rhythms, and see repeated geometric shapes like stair steps, all in bright colors. When in my thirties I described them to friends, they compared them to the visions induced by psychotropic drugs and said they sounded like fun. I found them frightening and not fun at all. But this evening's ecstatic audio experience had some of the same qualities as did drugs the doctor prescribed years ago for my headaches, a powerful combination of ergotamine and phenobarbitol. The primary difference was that this trip, although overwhelming, was pure pleasure.

As summer waned, the bullfrogs, like many of the birds, stopped singing. Crickets and coyotes continued. Seeds ripened and were eaten by the birds, or dropped to the ground, or flew through the air. At sun-down the low sun shone silver through sticky tar-weed, which had been flocked with dandelion and thistle fluff. Cracks in the earth widened; dust deepened. A robin hopped along a bare tractor path, fluffing her feathers in the dust. Brown fields lay beneath shimmering air. My lips chapped as maple and filbert leaves wilted.

Dirty and sweaty, I trudged up the dusty hill from the garden, popping blackberries into my mouth with hands stinking of fish fertilizer. Around the world were earthquakes and hurricanes, tsunamis, wars, famine, and disease. In my own nation, the then-administration seemed to have declared war on the environment. But at that moment I was selfishly and completely happy. The silk was on the corn; the sky was blue; a sweet breeze ruffled my hair; a wrentit trilled his bouncy song. Life was good.

By late August I generally begin to feel impatient with the heat, worry about wilted plants, both in the wild and in pots, and get very tired of watering. Then suddenly, I sense a bite in the night air. The sun seems a bit muted. Evening dew revives plants, which often get through the shorter day without my watering them though there is still no rain. Licorice ferns poke their fiddleheads through the moss on outstretched tree limbs and begin to unfurl.

As I water, I notice the color returning to the stems of red osier dogwood in nursery pots. The stems are red-brown or greenish in summer, but in an open sunny spot in winter, the young twigs are rendered an intense red. I asked a plant physiologist friend the reason for the fading and brightening, but he was not aware of it. I speculated the brightening might be caused by more direct sun reaching the bark as the leaves drop or, more likely, it is due to a chemical change caused by the shrub's preparation for dormancy. At first I wondered if I was imagining it because I didn't see it that early in the wild, where the foliage conceals the stems unless you're up close. But in my pots it was obvious—a tantalizing prelude to winter's glorious color that will be just as intense in the wild as it is in my pots.

PART FOUR

Fifteen Autumns

Chapter Fourteen

September mornings often find me picking a cup of blackberries to go with my breakfast. To me, blackberries epitomize the truth that there are few black-and-white answers in life. A good part of the year I spend swearing at their thorny, vigorous, rapidly spreading canes. If we didn't do regular battle with them, they would take over every sunny spot on the property. But at this time of year, how I do love their fruit.

Foraging meals from the land is tremendously satisfying to me, especially when the yield is sweet, fat, juicy blackberries. And blackberries stimulate myriad reminiscences. My mother loved Himalayan blackberries, the biggest and most invasive of the exotic brambles. She made pies and upside-down cakes, and canned dozens of quarts for winter and spring desserts.

Making a blackberry upside-down cake was the way I celebrated the end of World War II. My parents were at a rose show in Portland, about a hundred miles south of my hometown of Chehalis, Washington. I'm not sure where my sisters were, but my memory is that Grandfather and I were home alone. Mrs. Rand from next door ran over laughing and crying, barely able to get out the words.

"Did you hear? It was on the radio. It's over! The war is over!"

Elated to the point of giddiness, I longed to tell my parents, but I couldn't. I wanted to celebrate. But what could I do? Not yet ten years old, and living in a frugal wartime economy, celebrations I might think of now didn't occur to me. But I had to do something. Suddenly it hit. I grabbed a bucket and ran to the lower part of our acre, filling my pail with berries. The fragrance of a steaming blackberry upside-down cake and the news of the war's end greeted my parents on their return.

Decades later, my mother was in a wheelchair, twisted, crumbling, shrunken, her misery sculpted by rheumatoid arthritis and osteoporosis. My Aunt Mary pushed her up the driveway, talking in her warm, liquid voice, and stopped by a berry thicket. She gently stroked Mother's hair and then popped blackberries into her little sister's appreciative mouth. Mother liked them best when the central core was beginning to stain purple. That's when they were sweetest.

When our son Jeff was starting fourth grade, he and his friend Steve came to our empty house after school. David and I were at work and Erika was with friends. Common expectation might be for a couple of nine-year-old boys home alone to get into trouble. But what they did was to pick blackberries and make a pie, completely on their own. I don't remember whether they ate it on their own as well. After that it became a tradition for Jeff to make a pie every fall. After he went away to college, I always got an extra pang, missing him, at blackberry time.

More recently, our Sadie dog would join me as I grazed among the blackberries. She would pull back her lips and pick the berries with her teeth. She was very selective, picking only the ripe ones. Issa would watch as if that were a really odd thing to do, and then, because Sadie had done it, Issa would pick one or two as well. But she would often get pricked, and I'm not sure she thought the rewards were worth the effort.

For years Sadie and Issa hung out with us, tagging along on the blackberry harvest, running excitedly ahead when we went exploring, lying nearby when I watered or potted our plants. They were not only good company, they were working members of our nursery team. It was the dogs' job to keep the deer from devouring the plants. They did their job well until one year when Issa met her match. We were coming home from a walk and found a doe in a patch of garden near the gate. Issa charged the deer, who, instead of running, turned toward Issa, stood on her back legs and came crashing down. She lowered her head to thwack the impudent dog and something connected—the hooves or the head—not seriously, but frighteningly. Issa never chased another deer.

Then the dogs started getting old. Sadie's ears were the first to go. We would come home, and where was Sadie to greet us? A wonderful thing about dogs is that they don't have bad days and they don't carry grudges. However tired or grouchy you feel, your dog runs to welcome you, tail wagging and body wiggling in lieu of a smile. So it was a sad day when Sadie slept through our homecoming.

Shortly thereafter, Issa started having seizures or mini-strokes that would temporarily paralyze her. She always regained her mobility but with one attack she went blind—and that was permanent. At first she was terrified. She would flinch in fear when we touched her and recoil when she bumped into things. But, always tough and stubborn, she gradually accepted the challenge. Within about a week she began charging around fearlessly, guided, I suppose, by memory and smell. She came not only to accept our touch, but to seek it out, pushing her spotty head against our legs. She was a tremendous inspiration to me, one I will remember if I'm unlucky enough to lose my sight.

Sadie kept on puttering along, her same old deaf, sweet, smelly self. Her eyes grew cloudy but she seemed to adjust to the dimming light. When she was about a hundred and eight in people years, with increasing blindness and a bit of doggy Alzheimers, she began getting stuck in strange places. At 2 a.m. August 29, 2001, I pulled myself out of the depths of sleep hearing Sadie's plaintive calls. I'd been hearing them subconsciously for a while, but had no idea whether it was for five minutes or an hour. In my nightshirt and slippers, I followed the cries down the wood chip path, around the corner, and into the blueberry bushes. Soon I thought I made out a bit of white that could possibly be a dog. So I crawled under the blueberries until finally I saw her clearly. She stood stiff, statue-like, her legs entwined among the branches. I had to tug and pull to turn her in the right direction, but we finally got back into the house and to bed.

She continued her confused behavior, which had to be as frustrating to her as it was for us. She would get stuck under a chair or wrapped around a table leg, behind the stove, or simply with her nose against a wall. She seemed particularly restless at night, or perhaps it was just that I was around to hear her only at night. Her doleful *hnnnnn hnnnn hnnnnn* or more desperate *erk!* woke me repeatedly: 1 a.m. under a chair, 2:30 stuck beneath the bed, 3:15 outside, tangled in a rose bush.

I stopped at the grocery store before my day's activities in town on the morning of September 11, and was puzzled at the somber whispering among the clerks. At last I asked if there was a problem.

"An airplane flew into one of the Twin Towers in New York," my clerk said.

"How awful!" I responded. "Was there something wrong with its equipment?"

"They think it was on purpose," she said grimly.

I gasped, and asked for details, but she had none.

I'm not sure how I spent the day. I remember watching awful images on the television at the gym. I remember being in the park, walking in shock, crying and singing "America the Beautiful"—I, who was forever criticizing our administration, but who dearly loved this country. Childhood memories of distress and fear at the bombing of Pearl Harbor swirled in my head and in my gut. I assumed we were at war.

We spent the evening with friends, watching horrible replays and frightening speculation. Some estimated that fifty thousand had been killed. We went home late, disquieted, dazed, and exhausted, quite ready to fall into bed. But Sadie was nowhere to be found.

We thought she'd been safely confined, but somehow she had escaped. Blind, deaf, and confused, how could she have gone far? But if she was close, why couldn't we hear her? And if she'd strayed a long way, she'd never be able to find her way back. She had to be stuck somewhere, paralyzed with fright. Had someone picked her up? Was she even still alive?

We searched in the dark, but we have twenty-one wooded and brushy acres. How would we begin to guess where to look? We searched the mile stretch of road above and below our place. No sign. No sound. Already fatigued from nights of interrupted sleep before this emotionally draining day, we decided to try again in the morning, hoping Sadie too was sleeping somewhere.

I think I did sleep a little between images of the Twin Towers crumbling and Sadie trapped and crying. Around 3 a.m. I thought I heard her bark. I donned a head lamp and headed in the direction of the sound. I stumbled around in the dark for a while but heard nothing more. Had I dreamed her bark?

The next morning we turned the radio on to hear the latest news from New York and Washington D.C. We grabbed a quick breakfast and resumed our search. If she would just call, we could home in on her yelp. She always called. Why couldn't I hear her? We searched the road and the ditches, fearing she might have been hit, but we found nothing. We desperately wanted to call her, but it would have made little sense. She couldn't hear a thing—not a human voice calling nor a truck bearing down on her.

We scoured the area. We'd return to our house and listen to the radio as people searched the urban rubble for victims, and we'd go back out and search the woods and fields for Sadie. As I got increasingly worried and weary, the day took on a nightmarish quality. It felt as if I were looking for victims of the terrorist attack; the news on the radio was of people looking for Sadie. I felt numb and disoriented.

At one point I drove down to the bottom of the road and slowly back up, remembering the direction of the early-morning imagined sound.

Halfway up the hill, there it was again. I parked the car, excitedly climbed the fence into the neighbor's pasture and headed for a thicket under some oak trees. But once again, I neither saw nor heard any sign of Sadie.

Frustrated, I dashed home to get David. Surely between us we could find her. But once again, we were defeated. I willed her to bark. Still no sound. Nothing. I doubted myself again, but at the same time felt positive I'd heard her earlier. Eventually we decided to break for dinner.

After dinner I went back to the neighbor's oak woodland, determined to stay at least until dark. But before I was even off the road, I heard Sadie's unmistakable *Erk! Erk! Erk!* I scrambled over the fence and ran toward the sound, still seeing nothing. *Keep barking, Sadie! Keep barking!* As I got closer, I was incredulous to hear that the sound was coming from the middle of an immense sea of blackberry bushes, probably a quarter acre or more, with canes arching as high as my head. *How on earth did she get there?* I wondered. *And how will I?*

I glanced up at the house of our unfriendly, gun-owning neighbors. I couldn't see anyone and hoped that meant they couldn't see me. I turned my attention back to the blackberries. Wearing gloves but without tools, I had no choice but to use my body to force my way forward. Raising each foot higher than the opposite knee, I took giant steps, stomping down one thorny arching stem after another. I glanced toward the neighbor's house now and then, thinking about their teaching their dogs to attack strangers, and their favorite weekend entertainment—target practice. I was surprised but grateful that their dogs hadn't gone after Sadie. Perhaps it was the thorny thicket that had protected her.

Concentrating on keeping my balance, getting my foot high enough, not tripping or getting tangled, I made my way some fifteen feet into the brambles. Then in the dusk, with my foot poised in the air, ready to squash another stem, I saw her, just inches away, a black and white ball in a little pocket, down under the thorny stems and leaves.

She looked up at me but didn't murmur, and remained very still. She showed no emotion, neither fear nor happiness. But I was flooded with relief to find her not only alive, but apparently unhurt. With great effort I managed to move the berry canes off her, pick her up and find my way back through the thicket. I carried her up the hill, resting now and then and hoping she might walk, then picking her up again. David was astonished and delighted to see her. We each breathed gratified sighs when she eagerly drank water, and eventually ate as well.

We listened to the radio. I stroked Sadie and rejoiced for survivors, stroked Sadie and wept for those still searching and for those who had found their loved ones' remains. We were grateful when the toll of the missing was revised down and down again, but the total of nearly three thousand was still grotesque. All those people lost—and all those parents, children, sweethearts left alone. I longed to have my own children and grandchildren near, and buried my face in Sadie's fur.

Rather than being at war, we had been attacked by an organization. But instead of treating it as a criminal act and tracking down the perpetrators, our government chose to bomb a country. Now there would be more innocents lost, more weeping mothers and fathers, children, and lovers. Shocked and saddened by the attack, disconcerted by our country's response, I felt anxious and impotent.

You write letters to congresspeople, you demonstrate, but then what? Where do you go, what do you do, to quiet the buzzing head, aching gut, jittery nerves? I have a list of potential therapies: a hard workout at the gym, grubbing blackberries or running wild paths, writing with deep focus and concentration, and my ace-in-the-hole, exploring. In the out-of-doors, change is the constant and I can immerse myself in its present. Flowers open; fruit forms; leaves fall. Birds sing and nest and fly. Animals have babies and eat other animals and die and decompose. Each moment I drink in, breathe it into my head and heart and lungs. Each miraculous moment.

Chapter Fifteen

While summer seems to explode on the scene, fall tiptoes in one step at a time. We feel its bite in the night air as early as mid-August. By September chlorophyll begins fading from the leaves, inspiring me to name September's the Green-Leaking Moon. Ash leaves pale; poison oak reddens, its flaming foliage leaping over shrubs and licking up tree trunks. Fern gardens sprout through moss on tree branches, not waiting for the rain. And I'm suddenly aware of the local birds, the ones who keep us company year around.

As I filled flats with seedling mix one early-September morning, the fir tree above me sang—pizzicato and allegro—a whole choir of tiny voices. I looked up and saw only fir boughs and needles, branches covered with brown moss, spider webs. Finally I detected motion, followed by more and more as scores of diminutive birds moved so quickly I couldn't focus on them. Then a five-inch bird stopped and looked directly at me. I was surprised to see the white line separating his black yarmulke from the equally black eye mask. This was not our local black-capped chickadee, but a mountain chickadee, perhaps moving to a lower elevation for the winter.

Chickadees often travel in mixed flocks with kinglets and nuthatches, although they are so busy flitting through the brush, hanging upside down on twigs, exploring, gleaning, that I find them hard to distinguish unless I put aside my work and get out the binoculars. I've been able to spot an occasional kinglet, one with its bright orange crown exposed as it perched on the edge of a tub of water. Nuthatches I mostly notice from their toy-trumpet call in spring and summer, but I do catch occasional glimpses of them spiraling up or head-first-down a tree trunk. Nuthatches are surprisingly small birds for such resounding voices.

Around the time of fall equinox, the woolly-bear caterpillars begin lumbering across roads and walkways. Legend has it that the caterpillars, orange with a black mid-band, predict the winter's weather. But will winter be harsh when the black band is wider or when it's narrower than the orange? I can never remember. Most autumns the stripes seem about equal.

Either the spiders are more active in the fall, or their work is more apparent. One late-September day I counted three distinctly different forms of spider web over the course of a ten-minute walk. Webs looking like gauze hankies tossed helter-skelter littered the ditches and roadsides. Attached by corners and edges to blades of grass or bloomed-out flower stems, suspended like mini-trampolines, they were angled slightly, tipped down toward the home of the lurking predator. Cozy-looking, bread-loaf-shaped webs appeared to have been woven by homemakers like me and consisted of chaotic threads a bit like pulled-apart felt. I admired precisely woven, vertical orbs, attached horizontally or by radials to woody or herbaceous stems, often with the large weaver at home in the center of concentric rings. Webs are fascinating in themselves, and truly enchanting as they reflect changes in the weather: decked with rain or dew drops, sparkling with frost.

That first season we camped by the pond, as the summer waned I used the olive oil as my temperature gauge—in the mid-forties Fahrenheit, it became cloudy. The degree of cloudiness correlated with the degree of cold. The oil would turn solid before the temperature reached the mid-thirties.

With the oil completely solid one day, I was busy transferring paper accumulated at our camp site to the recycle bin when I came upon soft felty bits mixed with a confetti of colored paper. Lifting the apparent nest, I found a stack of empty egg cartons, some with irregular holes in the top. An adult mouse split out the back door while another stared with wild frightened eyes from the bottom of the brown grocery bag, beside the stack of cartons. I picked up a layer of bedding and six little noses poked through the holes on the top carton. It was well below freezing and I couldn't bring myself to toss the little critters out of their nest. Okay, guys, I said. You win for now. But as soon as the weather warms up, out you go, into the world to seek your fortunes. The early cold spell didn't last; the mice got to find new homes (if the owls didn't find them first), and a few days later I finished gathering paper to be recycled.

In October we moved the outdoor kitchen to the site of our proposed house in order to get better light. We plan to use solar heat when we build, so had picked the location with that in mind. But after a couple of weeks of the rain coming sideways and the kitchen contents blowing in the wind, I reluctantly gave up outdoor cooking. We continued to sleep comfortably in the tent, with temperatures sometimes below twenty, until mid November, when we regretfully took down the tent before we left to visit relatives. I felt I would have been content camping forever. Even with the cold and rain, I missed it. In following years we continued to join the throngs routinely migrating with the seasons—but in our case, only on our own property.

It was in October of 2001 that we submitted land-use plans, building plans, and a couple of fat checks to the county to begin the permit process for our new home. And we began clearing brush and cutting small trees to satisfy the fire-break requirements. The following February some overworked official finally found the time to look at our forms, and approved the land-use application—the permission to apply for a building permit. But the county wouldn't consider the building permit application until the fire break had been approved, the fire department had endorsed the construction of the driveway, and a drain-field had been installed. When we invited the fire chief out he had few comments on the drive but recommended we install a sprinkler system in the house.

"It will take twenty minutes for the trucks to reach you," he said. "Your house could be ashes by then."

We asked him how he thought we were doing on the fire break and he was non-committal. "Fires rarely start in the trees around here," he said. "It almost always begins inside the house."

That wasn't awfully reassuring, but at least it gave us hope that the fire-break inspection might not be as rigorous as we had feared. So we invited the county inspector out. He smiled, said, "You're on the right track. Keep up the good work," and left.

We didn't want to be on the right track. We wanted to be done. But there it was. The county required thirty feet of virtual desert around the house, and another one hundred feet nearly clear, with any trees widely spaced. I had been fighting that all along, which made clearing more difficult for David. I had moved to the woods because I wanted to live in the woods, not in a desert. And I wanted thickets and trees with flowers and fruit for the wildlife. We were discouraged, and with the nursery and track meets, very busy. We put our permit preparations on the back burner.

Eventually we got back to it and discovered our original application period had run out. More money got us reinstated. We heard that the local Audubon Society had met with the county to stress that, while taking care to avoid obvious fuel sources, preserving wildlife habitat was essential. Was it naïve to hope that might make a difference for us? We hired a logger friend for some strategic thinning. We (mostly David) cleared blackberries that had returned since our last inspection. We cut and pruned and sawed, called the inspector and held our breath.

The inspector was complimentary about the fuel break but his assistant noted a couple of places where the driveway was six inches to a foot too narrow. So then it was more grading, more loads of gravel, a few more thousand dollars, lots of measuring. We walked the drive with a twelve-foot-long pole to measure the width and then held it vertically at knee-height to check overhead clearance. The inspector's assistant had made it clear that a width of eleven and a half feet would not pass. And just in case, we wanted to insure that no branch would be an inch lower than the requisite fourteen feet overhead! We sawed; we mowed; we hauled and raked gravel. A fire-department inspector came out to approve the expensive super-highway-driveway, followed by yet another visit from the county inspector. And finally, six years from when we started the process, our building-permit application could move forward.

Western Oregon is known for its rain but the rainy season has been slow in coming the past few years. Most falls, filbert leaves are big gold snowflakes clustering and swirling in the air. But in years when there is little rain in September or October, they hang from their twigs like limp dirty rags far into the fall. I look uneasily at desiccated foliage that refuses to color or to drop. But even in such years, the rains eventually begin, distressing sun worshipers and those outdoor workers who object to mud and wet socks, but gratefully welcomed by myriad thirsty mouths beneath the soil and in the cells of leaves. It *pok pok tic ticka tak taks* on the metal roof of the trailer and on the tent and on the canvas top of the shelter that covers our outdoor kitchen. *Pok pok ticka ticka* builds to become the sound of one hundred hands clapping. Then *crash!* go the cymbals, *boom!* goes the bass drum, and the timpani roll. Abruptly the drum solo stops, and it's back to *ticka ticka pok pok.* Or more often, the percussionist stays home, and the crescendo is minimal, but the smattering of applause from a small appreciative audience continues.

When fall rains come heavy, the drops big and warm, I have memories of my childhood. Energized by the rare warm rain, Mother would call us and excitedly help us out of our clothes. We would bolt naked into the celestial shower, running, shouting, jumping, and lifting our mouths to the pouring heavens. Through the years I would occasionally mention my suppressed urge during a particularly inviting downpour, eliciting raunchy responses from nearby males. I learned that we not only don't indulge, we don't even talk about it. So it was with a special joy that, listening to the rain on the tent roof one recent fall morning, I hit on how to get the approximate quarter-mile to the house without getting my clothes wet. I hollered at David as I ran laughing by our outdoor kitchen, my clothes bundled in my arms—sharing the fun, perhaps, or maybe just releasing my inner exhibitionist.

I'll call October's moon the Fungus Moon or Sour Blackberry Moon or Beginning-of-the-Rain Moon or Golden-Foliage Moon.

"The color has never been this good," we exclaim during the golden days of most any October. Low sun bathes deciduous leaves in golden light, reflected back by the flaxen coin-sized foliage of snowberries and sarvisberry, the mid-sized ochre leaves of filbert and cascara, and the immense clear yellow big-leaf maple, the voluptuous blond of the forest whose leaves can measure as much as eighteen inches across. Native crabapple glows cranberry-juice red in the sun and clear bright yellow in the shade. Scattered saffron rays suffuse the woodland, startling against dark tree trunks and nearly black foliage of the conifers. Golden leaves float down singly or in twos and threes. Then a gust brings a rush and swirl of maybe one hundred.

Slant-wise light shines on emerald moss carpets, which remain lush from the time the first fall rains come until summer's heat bakes away their green. Once I walked in the woods with my then five-year-old granddaughter Tasha, who delighted in the soft bright green moss. "Oh!" she exclaimed. "This would be a wonderful place for a wedding!" Deeper in the woods the young firs were so dense that their lichen-draped lower limbs were dead, and little grew on the heavily shaded ground. Her eyes got big. "This looks like where the wicked witch lives," she said.

Coming down from our hill, we travel through narrow valleys whichever direction we go: north to Veneta, population about four thousand, or south to the unincorporated community of Lorane, or east to Eugene. On an early October day we follow sinuous gold streams of ash trees protecting Coyote and Fox Hollow creeks. Beyond the waterways clear yellow, lime yellow, and bronze mounds of deciduous trees, punctuated by black-green Douglas fir spires, clothe hillsides logged decades earlier and allowed to regenerate naturally. Elsewhere, clear-cut patches and stubbly tracts of newly planted firs alternate with sections of young fir plantation that look like green wide-wale corduroy. Where hills rise abruptly, maple trunks lean toward the road, their dark boughs forming a canopy of gold over our heads.

On our hill (and doubtless others as well, but this is where I walk), on fall days after a rain, the soft-body creatures take to the road—a sure route to assisted suicide. Newts, frogs, snakes, and especially our big native slugs seem intent, like the chicken, to reach the other side. Walking down the road toward our drive, I rescue yet another banana slug—six inches long and the color of an old banana, complete with black splotches—from the middle of the road. Honoring its chosen direction of travel, I deposit its slimy body gently on a mossy bed under a maple tree. "Stay in the woods, you silly thing," I instruct it. I carry two more to safety, this time of the olive-green kind I call dill-pickle slugs, thinking that it's too bad I can't tag them so that I would know if I kept foiling the suicide attempts of the same individuals.

A few minutes later I turn into our driveway and without missing a step, stomp an exotic snail. My Inner Nag notes that I refrain from looking down at the swiftly dispatched remains. She looks askance and asks, "Where is all this peace and love and acceptance I keep hearing about?"

I get defensive. "It's different," I explain, to no one in particular. "That's the brown garden snail and it doesn't belong here. It's not part of our ecosystem. It's destructive. People brought these pests here without their natural enemies, so it's up to people to combat them." And then I imagine a gargantuan foot coming from somewhere above me, aimed directly for my exotic head.

Farther along the driveway the first shaggy-mane mushrooms push columnar colonies through the compacted gravel. About four inches long, rice-paper white and decorated with rough tan scallops, these are said to have a delicious, delicate flavor and excellent texture when gathered young. But they must be picked early and eaten quickly, because as they mature, they deliquesce to a thick black ink. This is their way of dispersing their spores. One day the mushroom will be firm and roughly egg shaped. The next day the edge will spread and curl back to a bell-shape, its lower edge scalloped and dripping. In another day or two, depending on the weather, all that will remain is a stem in a murky pool. Enzymes dissolve the mushroom tissue, pulling the gills apart to discharge spores to the air. Although they end in a black puddle, shaggy manes emerge with such strength that, according to mushroom expert David Aurora, they can burst through asphalt. He says one was recorded to have lifted a ten-pound slab of concrete.

When the weather turns moist in the early fall, mushrooms abound. Turkey tails, puff balls, lavender to violet *Russulas*, mushrooms of pink, black, tomato-soup red, yellow; ghostly white, striped, and translucent mushrooms. David and I gather chanterelles in the fall and morels in the spring but don't feel confident enough to go beyond admiring most of the others.

Now and then in the fall the wind blusters. After a good gust the driveway becomes a collage, and each item has a story. Twigs and branches dressed in lichen and moss harbor tiny insects dined on by birds. Leathery round-lobed leaves of the white oak tell this region's history. Its acorns were a major food for local Kalapuya, and Oregon white oak was the primary tree in the Willamette Valley and foothills when European Americans first arrived. Farming, development, and the decision not to continue the Indians' tradition of burning, have seriously depleted oak ecosystems, both savannahs and woodlands, endangering a multitude of plants and animals dependent on them. I welcome our oak trees and protect them jealously. Mixed among the white oak leaves are pointy-toothed black oak leaves, which I'm also happy to see. This is the northern edge of black oak's range. In southern Oregon and northern California, where they are more prevalent, they have been getting a disease brought in from Europe with the descriptive name "sudden oak death." Perhaps these northerly individuals will help maintain the species.

Scrambled in with the oak leaves on the driveway are other representatives of the woodland: oceanspray, osoberry, crabapple, and big-leaf maple. Fine filaments of pale greenish-gray *Usnea,* the lichen that drapes trees in elongated leis or beards of gray (often called Spanish moss, although it is neither Spanish nor moss), lie among the leaves. We also find the lush, leaf-like lichens *Lobaria* and *Peltigera*, whose upper surfaces are gray-green, bright green, gray, or brown, with whitish lower surfaces. Many of these lichens are pollution sensitive and are therefore disappearing from much of the world, so it's a special thrill to see them.

Evolutionarily ancient, lichens are composite organisms containing a fungus and a photosynthesizing partner that is either an alga, a cyanobacteria, or both. Nature guides explain to children that the fungus makes the house and the alga makes the food, the fungal partner providing a surface to capture mineral elements from rain, dew, and fog and to protect the photosynthesizing partner from the drying sun and wind. Leafy lichens illustrate the partnership well, with the distinctive paler fungal side and darker photosynthesizing side. Cyanobacteria can fix atmospheric nitrogen to a form usable by plants; as the rain leaches it or as the lichen decomposes, it contributes greatly to forest fertility. One kind of leafy lung lichen, *Lobaria oregana*, contributes most of the nitrogen necessary for the growth of old coniferous forests in the western Cascades.

Acting for the forest canopy as a mulch does for a garden, lichens hold moisture and intercept nutrients that would otherwise be lost or unavailable, releasing them to the forest. Lichen crusts on barren soils can make the difference between a soil that will hold water and nutrients and one from which nutrients and soil will wash away.

Lichens provide food, shelter, and nesting material for wildlife. Mammals from elk to mice eat them. Some lichens are even considered survival food, although it's good to note the advice of a sage who suggests that "parboiling with an old pair of hiking boots might improve the flavor." Some are a source of poison, so, as with mushrooms, we don't just munch randomly.

The moisture and coolness of fall bring other surprises as well. I like to walk at night on our property or up the road, and I prefer not to use a flashlight, whose big glowing circle limits my eyes and my mind to the confines of its halo. I want to see trees and night birds silhouetted against the sky. I want to see clouds and stars and moon. I want to see the night.

I have taken some spectacular spills, walking in the dark. Several times I've strayed from the path into brambles or the ditch. Once I slammed my toe into the butt end of a log and crashed down hard on the log pile. That convinced me to carry a flashlight, but I leave it tucked in my pocket, to use only in case of a dire emergency.

Before I began carrying an emergency light, I took a walk to the pond on a moonless fall night. As dark as it was, the gnarly oak branches and shaggy forms of Douglas firs were darker still against the night sky.

Beyond them, the stars shone with an intense brilliance. I walked gazing at the sky, marveling at the spectacle, until I had to drop my eyes to the ground to relax my cramped neck. Much to my astonishment, there on the ground I saw another star. I gasped at its radiance. Initially I thought this glittering object was reflecting light from another source, but there was no light anywhere to be reflected. It couldn't be, of course, but to me it looked exactly like a tiny fallen star. And then I found another, and another. Surely Tinkerbell had floated through, scattering stardust along my path. As my excitement built, my curiosity swelled along with it. I couldn't imagine what sort of wonderland I had stumbled into.

I was surrounded by minute dazzling dots, glimmering embers glowing not red, but silver. "White hot," I remember from childhood, is much hotter than "red hot." I was sure I would be burned if I touched one, but I had to discover the reality of these twinkling mysteries. Finally I screwed up the courage to pick one up, scooping up a good handful of forest duff beneath it to protect my hand. To my surprise I felt no heat, but the gleam remained constant. Having many times singed my fingers on incandescent light bulbs, I thought our engineers could learn a lot from whatever I was carrying: imagine such brilliance without energy being lost to heat!

Nearly hyperventilating, I rushed my treasure into the trailer. Once under the lantern light, the starlight was extinguished. I was amazed to see, cupped in my hand, a brownish half-inch worm. This had to be a glowworm, but in all the years I'd lived around here, I had never seen one. I always understood glowworms to be the larval form of fireflies (which are actually beetles, not flies), but we don't have fireflies out here. So the mystery needed further solving.

With the help of an Oregon State University entomologist I learned that, though we indeed don't have fireflies in Oregon, we do have glowworms. This is a different species from the winged beetles that light the nights elsewhere. Here the larvae glow, and the female, who retains the larval form even after reaching reproductive maturity, continues to be luminescent. Adult males, not surprisingly, are attracted to light and, in their beetle form, fly to the side of the flashing female. Different species of glowworms send different patterns of light, and sometimes a female, hungering less for sex than for nourishment, will signal a "foreign" male, and when he comes courting he becomes her dinner. (Which may be only a good story. References I've read more recently say adults probably don't eat at all.)

I felt particularly fortunate in finding my path star-strewn. Glowworms are uncommon here and becoming more so as land is developed and pesticides become more prevalent. I was delighted to discover that some glowworms are predators of slugs and snails. Exotic gastropods, particularly the European brown garden snail, which was introduced to California by an enterprising chef dreaming of a fortune in escargot, are the ruin of many of my nursery plants. So now I've been introduced to a helper—and to another reason, besides protection of the birds, reptiles, and mammals, for not using toxic slug bait. After all, who would want to snuff out the stardust?

One fall day while wandering in the woods I came upon a fir log that David had cut from a wind-damaged tree. It was maybe three feet across, lying near the stump. Its deeply fissured bark showed that it was not young, and counting the rings, I realized it was about the same age as I am, my bark wrinkled as well. The rings held its autobiography. This circle of wood was laid down in a droughty year: rings tight together showed minimal growth. Later circles showed good years, putting on ample wood to separate the rings widely. Here trauma caused off-center growth and, farther out, dark arrow-shaped wood and a distorted ring testified to the loss of an early branch.

I thought how like a tree a person is. The years are all there. That seedling and sapling are still inside, ring upon ring—long-ago events, old influences, all part of today's being. Here is the ring from the second grade when you ran to school, on the edge of tears, worrying you might be late. You came upon a little girl crying beside her over-turned wagon. When you stopped to right it for her, her big eyes, surprised smile, and dried tears sped you happily on your way to school—your first lesson that helping someone else helps the self at least as much. The fourth-grade ring holds the outcast's misery when everyone you knew was excitedly planning something to which you were clearly excluded. Weeks of pain culminated in your own surprise birthday party and the discovery that emotional responses have far more to do with perception than with fact.

A few rings later your father told you that you couldn't assume higher morality in someone just because of their uniform, clerical robes, or profession, and you were awakened to the fact that people are pretty much people however they look, whatever they do. The eighth-grade ring instructed that the *terra* was not necessarily *firma* when a magnitude

7 earthquake in western Washington rolled the ground like waves in the sea. Here is the distortion from the loss of your parents. Here is another from the loss of a friend.

All those years, those accumulated rings, give the tree its strength and direct its growth. They comprise what it becomes and record the history of where it has been. As I looked at it lying there, thinking of the story of its life, I wondered if inside its wrinkled skin its heart didn't still feel like that of a sapling.

Chapter Sixteen

It was in the fall of 1998 that our son Jeff, his eyes brimming, told us that he and his wife were splitting up. I spent a teary, wakeful night grieving for him, for our grandchildren, and finally for ourselves. We were losing the woman David had so fondly called his "blue-nosed daughter-in-law" during a lucid moment in Intensive Care. David was sad and confused, hurt for Jeff, and a bit angry. We talked and probed and searched for explanations. In our vulnerable state and with whatever heightened senses our half-decade of quiet had brought us, we awakened to our own buried piques and misunderstandings.

As I've analyzed it in retrospect, before we moved to the woods, neither of us had been willing to acknowledge the flaws in our personal pictures of the perfect life. David had undoubtedly dreamed of a brilliant architectural career. He is a fine designer, but I don't believe he had counted on querulous clients, uncollected bills, conflict with colleagues. My own vision was of a family playing, backpacking, cycling, discussing, and creating in joyful harmonious togetherness. When David drowned his frustrations in brew, I took it personally. When I realized we were four individuals with individual goals, I went looking outside the family for my fulfillment—and David took it personally. Neither of us had learned to share feelings that might offend the other. So each was quietly stung, unaware of the distress of the other.

Living out in the woods we learned to see life as it is, not as we might dream it or see it on T.V. We became less caught up in ourselves and more tuned in to the world. We began to see each other, along with the bugs and flowers and voles, as what we each were: our contributions, habits, needs—not good or bad, just there. Pieces of life. Part of the whole.

One night years later when David was long asleep, I slipped between the sheets. Reaching toward him, I realized he was lying on the top sheet. I could feel his form and his warmth but couldn't touch him. In a few hours he awoke sufficiently to climb under the sheet. I sleepily threw my leg over his and he pulled me close. I thought of how that reflected the difference between our lives in the country and in town. In "civilization," meetings, the pub, television, not discussing concerns, eventually wove a membrane between our parallel lives. Each recognized the other's form and could even feel the warmth, but often could not reach across the barrier. In our woods, without those escapes and distractions, and with the impetus of having discussed the dissolution of Jeff's marriage, the barrier dissolved. Although we had nursed our own hurts, each was surprised and chagrined at the other's. We laughed and cried and said, "Oh, I'm so sorry." We hugged and promised to keep talking—and listening.

Renewed romance is fabulous, but I appreciated at least as much the melting of the membrane of dis-union. We found each other. And we regained trust. We felt twinges of guilt that our new level of happiness seemed to emerge from our son's sorrow, and were frustrated at not being able to help him. But as I write this eight years later, our grandchildren's lives are full and rewarding; their mother has realized considerable success with her art and is in a happy relationship; Jeff, a respected teacher and coach at one of Oregon's finest high schools, is in love with Rachel, a magnetic teacher from across town; and David and I are still on our honeymoon.

On the way to town on a November morning, fog splashes and gusts against my windshield as I drive through cloud after earth-bound cloud. In the valley the fog hangs in thin horizontal sheets. In some places it makes pools and lakes that scattered tree-islands pop through. In the distance it is a Japanese painting in which trees are silhouetted against ever-more misty layers of trees.

The air is filmy, soft, gentle as a caress. A scene unfolds that moves me so, I want to share it with the world. In the foreground stands a heavy-trunked oak tree, bole and branches dark with moss, green-tinged gray fluffs of lichen scattered along the trunk and throughout the tree to a foot or so from the crown. The crown itself is a canopy of caramel, aglow in the rays of the angled sun. More moss-covered tree trunks, the gold foliage of smaller trees, sporadic red-leafed dogwood and crabapple grow behind and adjacent to the oak. Garlands of silvery *Usnea* adorn the trees, with lichens, moss, scarlet and golden foliage shimmering in the low light before dark Douglas fir, all softened by the drifting vaporous veil.

Some days the fog is so dense I can't see beyond the first tree, fifteen feet or so in front of me. I could be alone on earth, living in a cloud. No hills, no houses are visible. I like the mystery of the fog and the impressionistic beauty it brings, but when it lasts day after day it seems to seep under the door like poison gas, under your clothes and into your bones. But then one day it begins to thin. Patches of blue sky and the tops of neighboring hills appear. Fog floats in drifts and billows like steam from a teakettle. Looking down the hill through dark tree trunks and golden leaves, soon I can see the pasture below and, beyond that, the road, scattered houses, and the distant hills. I am no longer isolated. I am part of a community, a countryside, a world.

I think I'll call November's the Fog Moon.

Fall is when animals' harvest and storage of food picks up urgency and plants undergo quiet, beneath-the-ground changes as they too store food in roots and rhizomes, preparing for a burst of life in the spring. Being in the late autumn of my life, I feel particularly akin to this time of year. Our grandchildren are spring's promise and potential. Camila at age five is the energy of bulbs pushing through the ground, the innocence and awakening of soft new growth. Ten-year-old Tasha is swelling leaf buds, flowers opening, twigs strengthening. With their teen years behind them, Celina and Nate's leaves spread wide to the sun, their roots thirsty and seeking, flowers blooming full in the knowing of summer's approach.

Our children, Erika and Jeff, are reaping the fullness of summer. Flowers, fruit, branches, and foliage expand ever richer, substance and vigor building to a grand crescendo. And we, as the plants store and re-allocate their summer's products, we gather what we have gleaned through the years, sorting, analyzing, weighing, assimilating, and re-distributing.

I often wind my memory tape back to the day Erika and I stood beside David's hospital bed, looking out the window. "They think what they're doing is so important," Erika had said, as we watched the miniature people far below rushing from place to place. And I ask myself what I consider important. As David got his health back, my answer to that question was "my family." I felt that, having found the answer, I should act on it, although I wasn't sure what that meant. I tried briefly to insinuate myself into my children's lives, but that was a non-starter. They are mature, competent, independent. It made no sense for them or for me to inject myself into their worlds. They needed to be independent; they needed me to be independent; I needed me to be independent. So I searched further. Eventually, as I explored in our hills and got better acquainted with my fellow travelers, both plant and animal, it occurred to me that I was thinking too small. My family doesn't stop with my husband and our bloodline, but includes all of the species so necessary for the earth's health.

Those connections have been revealed to me in many ways over a long period. One incident I particularly remember dates from Erika's first stay in France, when she was about twenty-three. It was the first time she had been so far away and I was lonesome for her. One night as I was feeling blue and gazing at the moon, it came into my head that, from the other side of the world, she was looking at the same moon (though not at the same moment). The thought was very comforting. Later I applied the same reasoning to friends and other family members, bringing them close even when they were far away. Eventually I made the next step to my unknown family—my sisters and brothers in Israel and Palestine, Afghanistan and Iraq, Jakarta and Darfur—all living their lives under the same changing moon, binding us all together.

As I learn more about the complexity of inter-relations, the web of family broadens. I love getting a glimpse into the essential world of microorganisms and appreciate them as the *sine qua non* of us all. Recently I was delighted to hear that the tangle of relationships goes on inside as well as outside our bodies. A pathologist speaking on the radio said many scientists feel that the mitochondria, the center of intracellular enzyme activity—and perhaps other structures in our bodies as well—evolved from bacteria. He said that he personally considers them still to be bacteria, just no longer free living. Even more amazing, of the thousands of cells in our body, microbiota comprise ten times the number of cells we could consider purely human. The pathologist said that he thinks of himself as more of an ecosystem than an individual, with all those microorganisms, captured or otherwise, relating to each other and to the body's chemistry and organs. Such a concept is exciting to me. I've never been comfortable with the idea of humankind being something apart from nature, something elevated and haughty. A great gift of our time in the woods has been the opportunity to see ourselves as small parts of an astonishingly complex scheme and now to see that complex scheme to be part of us as well.

By December the trees are mostly bare. Hillside costumes have changed from green and gold to woolly puffs among dusky spires, rounded forms of lichen-covered oak and maple contrasting with the dark points of Douglas fir. Up close, *Quercus garryana,* the Oregon white oak, becomes *Quercus rex* or perhaps *Quercus majesticus,* standing noble and august, robed in winter's royal garb. Warmly clothed in green-gold fur, his brawny silver-draped arms outstretched, he surveys his kingdom.

December's might be the Regal Oak Moon. Alternatives could be Calling-Owls Moon, Lichen Moon, or perhaps Running Waters Moon.

If the rains haven't already started in earnest, they do now. The pond fills; heavily trod paths run like rivers; streams overflow. We come home from town at night to find "Lake Fox-Coyote" at the confluence of Coyote Creek and Fox Hollow creek, the road at Gillespie Corners having disappeared under water that backs up across acres of pastureland. Ducks and geese paddle on what was dry land and neighbors put up signs proclaiming "Waterfront Property." The road usually reappears soon, but water often lingers in the fields. In 1859, long before the roads were banked and culverts installed, Lane County's first bridge was built at Gillespie Corners, allowing buggies and stage coaches to travel Territorial Road in a rainy winter without having to ford Coyote Creek. In the winter of 1996, after torrential rains, many rivers flooded; there were numerous mud slides, and at least one road dropped an amazing twenty feet overnight. But the next day skies were clear and blue and our souls were warmed by the sun.

The red sticky clay that makes up most of our hills makes you inches taller after the rain, as layer after layer of mud lifts the soles of your boots. The sun barely peeks over the horizon on these truncated days. I glory in its light effects and worship its rare warmth. Long before the solstice I ardently anticipate the sun's return. Some years ago my father-in-law pointed out that although solstice is the longest night of the year, the days don't lengthen evenly: afternoons get longer several weeks before mornings do. This information intrigued and delighted me. Each year since then I have watched the weather statistics and counted the days like a child waiting for Christmas.

Before the end of the first week in December, the sun reaches its earliest setting, at 4:34 in the afternoon. It holds more or less steady (seconds undoubtedly changing) until December 13, when it sets at 4:35. Hooray! We've gained a minute of afternoon daylight! Sunrise, however, keeps getting later. On December 22, the shortest day, the sun rises at 7:45 and sets at 4:38. By December 29, sunrise comes an additional three minutes later and holds there until January 8, when—*ta dah!*—it rises a minute earlier, at 7:47, making it a minute easier to get up on a dark morning.

One recent December gave me another return to celebrate. Since January of 1954, when I first met David as a college freshman, until May of 1995, he had worked on spatial problems with pencil and paper. He would work out designs for jobs or redesign some aspect of the house we were living in, or illustrate a concept he had thought of. He designed a remodel for our house in town and, before the work was completed, began re-remodeling the remodel on paper. He had our proposed house in the Lorane hills designed long before we moved here, but abandoned it when he realized his design would necessitate removing a big-leaf maple. He immediately completed a new design, but after his hemorrhage, it lay untouched.

David had come back to full function in most ways. His spatial orientation returned within a year, as did his physical strength and coordination. Other synapses slowly began to fire until the only remaining losses appeared to be his memory about the weeks following his hemorrhage and his architectural abilities. My unscientific theory is that an architect needs a left-brain-right-brain crossover to understand mathematical and engineering problems as well as aesthetic and artistic ones, and the particular neurons facilitating that crossover had not reconnected. The doctor gave little encouragement we'd see improvements after about a year and a half. But in December 2000, more than five and a half years after his hemorrhage and with no fanfare, David got out the old drawings he had begun all those years before. For days he only looked at them. To my eyes, he seemed anxious, and unwilling to pick up the pencil. Later he told me he just needed to read the drawings and remember. Early in 2001 he began drawing, rather matter-of-factly, as if there had been no hiatus. I was thrilled beyond telling. He was back. He was drawing. The architect's brain was re-connected.

Someone exclaimed, "Oh wonderful! Now you can get your house built!" Well, maybe. And that would be nice. But my excitement was not for that potential product, but rather because David's brain had re-learned what it was meant to do. He had been made whole.

Through the years I have sometimes despaired that David and I are too much dreamers and not enough doers. If dreams were carpenters, our house would be built. Clearly we must eventually build something, unless our personal decomposition out-paces that of the trailer. But I have come to the realization that, if I had to choose, I'd live here in a tent rather than in a house in town. I'm not sure about David. He doesn't indulge in that sort of speculation. For a decade and a half he has never lost faith that when the time is right, we will build our house.

As autumn wanes and solstice approaches, I might dread the coming of a dreary winter. But instead I see signs of rebirth. I admire the native filbert, its tight pink or beige catkins firm and straight or curved in crescents, dozens of elfin penises hanging out to dry, almost ready for assembly. I celebrate swelling leaf buds on osoberry and red-flowering currant. Leaves on the little herbaceous snow queen perkily await their early bloom. I joyously welcome the lengthening of daylight and the previews of a new cycle at the same time that I try to take personally the model, if not for hibernation, at least for a respectful winter-quiet mind and body in order to earn spring's renewal. But while I relax along with the dormant plants and admire the structure of leafless trees, I remember my father saying that their nakedness, along with the below-ground retreat of herbaceous plants, looked to him like death.

PART FIVE

Fifteen Winters

Chapter Seventeen

Our old half-Dalmatian Issa continued a gutsy full-speed-ahead life in her dark world through the fall of 1998. In the early winter I was distressed to discover bloody diarrhea. Soon she refused food, but even then, never complained. I couldn't imagine she was getting much joy out of life. Reluctantly, we called the vet to help her go. As we caressed her and told her we loved her, the vet inserted the needle and Issa relaxed.

We had been told that other pets often have trouble with the death of a member of their animal family, so when we returned from the vet we let Issa "lie in state" under the card table in our living room for a couple of days. Sadie and Caesar hovered, watched, and sniffed and then seemed satisfied. We dug a grave and lined it with moss, covered her with fern fronds and forest soil, and planted a dogwood tree above her.

Death is a conundrum. One moment a living creature lies on the table; the next there is only a body. The life—spirit? soul?—has floated away. The body decomposes and is recycled—that much is apparent. But what becomes of the spirit itself? The essence of life? Surely it must recycle as well.

Compost has brought me closer to the idea of reincarnation than religion ever did. My parents took us to church, believing that it was good for children to be brought up in a community where the cohesive message was of love, thoughtfulness, gratitude for blessings. But they were not at all doctrinaire. Daddy was agnostic in the truest sense of the word. He was an extremely moral man but he based his decisions and right behavior on consideration of others, on logic, and on the law. He lived according to the Golden Rule, but if scripture influenced that decision, it was a subconscious residue from childhood. He spoke of doing what was right, not what was written. We would spend the ride home from church dissecting the sermon.

Mother was religious but adhered to no particular church's teachings. She was definitely a deist. She saw God in nature. From the time we were very little she taught us "God is love." Which, whether or not that was her intent, I turned around to "Love is God." The core of goodness throughout the world, that basic spirit that is the path to peace, the path to justice, is love, is God.

My gardening mother believed in recycling long before it was publicly espoused, and believed equally in compost. She wrote of wanting her bones to "feed one lovely rose or help a fragrant lily grow" or "roll on the ocean floor or bleach in the desert sun … just so they return to the earth."

I am inspired by the rich soil that microorganisms make from organic matter: Recycling, reorganization, reincarnation, renewal. Nothing is wasted; nothing new is created. All that was dead lives again in a perpetual cycle. I believe that living so close to nature and watching its progression has helped me accept the idea of death. Death seems as natural as night—and then a new day dawns. I will die and the rhythms of the world—of night and day, of spring and fall—won't change at all. And what of me? The molecules and minerals and electrons will reorganize and carry on, but I don't have any reason to believe they'll organize in any sentient form. It will be fine to feed a carrot, if that is my future, but thinking about it does give me a push to do now whatever I really care about. It may not be possible as a carrot, or the carrot's predator, rabbit or radical.

I'm often reminded of a college conversation. I was fussing about something I wanted to do but didn't have the time, or perhaps it was money I didn't have enough of—I rarely had much to spare of either. A friend listened for a while, then he exploded, "This is your *life*, Evelyn! It's not some goddamn dress rehearsal!" Through the years, I think often of his words. And of course it's true that I have limited time. Don't we all? Getting more and more limited every day.

As I try to live consciously each moment, I also think about life's corollary. The one sure thing about life is its end. What is it they say? "You'll never get out of here alive!" I fantasize living full tilt until some prescribed moment when I invite family and friends to a *bon voyage* party, ask their leave, and say good-bye. While I'm at it, I'd like to note and record the dimming of the light—or the brightening of a new one.

I am aware that many deaths are far less kind. My father's bone cancer gave him tremendous pain but he was alert and joking until morphine increased his somnolence and a stroke stole away his speech. Mother, a fiercely independent woman, had all physical freedom stripped from her more than a dozen years before her death, her brittle bones and swollen, throbbing joints denying her the ability even to feed herself, much less stand or walk alone. Her mind remained sharp, quite able to remind her of all she couldn't do, trapped within her crumbling prison of pain. I pray

I will be able to go and go and go and then stop. Just like that. Death itself doesn't frighten me. I'm happy to add to Earth's compost.

But I've discovered that as is often the case, theory and the practical world are not necessarily in lock step. "That'll do to tell," my mother used to say, when our proclamations didn't match our behavior. I'm happy with the idea of adding to the Earth's compost but I'm in no hurry. I had some real moments of panic a few years back, as I went to get a mammogram report I was pretty sure was bad. When my suspicions were confirmed I sought the comfort of the decomposition cycle, but my Inner Judge attacked:

Oh you lie, woman! You lie! If you are so mellow and acquiescing and one with Mother Earth, what was that white-hot lightning bolt that tore through your chest, filling the void and searing the lining? What was the flaming torch you felt when you heard the diagnosis, "malignant"?

"Not a lie," I protested, once the fires subsided and the pounding bosom stilled. "A difference of opinion. Who among us is of one mind?"

The neocortex has no doubt, but the limbic system is disinterested in the philosophical. It clings to the moment—the eating, drinking, seeing, feeling, loving moment. I want to know more of this beautiful world's myriad species and processes. I want to watch my grandchildren develop and grow. I'm not afraid of death. But not now, oh Lord. Not now.

A terrifying day in the hospital feigning calm, quizzing nurses about their children, doctors about their technology; breathing intentionally, deeply, with studied control, culminated with the small malignancy being cleanly removed. The doctor recommended radiation with or without chemotherapy, but I opted out. I've lived through the Green Revolution and all the wonder poisons designed to make farming more productive, through miracle drugs to rid us of disease, and I've seen drug-resistant super-bugs created, and people dying from analgesics. I had a friend whose heart was burned with radiation and another whose final months were miserable from radiation-induced sickness. If this cancer had been bigger or more aggressive or if I had been much younger, I probably would have made a different decision. But as things were, I preferred to encourage my immune system rather than to poison it. Once I made that decision, it was not hard to put the whole matter aside. It made no sense to me to worry about cancer. I'm at least as likely to die in a car accident and I continue driving without anguishing about frightening possibilities. After the surgery, my only moments of distress came when the oncologist, who didn't appreciate my choice against radical treatment, said, "If the cancer returns, you *will die.*"

Stunned by the comment, I had no response, and my eyes filled. Later I wished I had said, "Yes, and if the cancer *doesn't* return I will die. And so will you, you bastard."

I suppose there will always be a collision between loving life and accepting death. But I intend to make my life as lovable as possible as long as I am able.

I'm far more comfortable with my reincarnation as compost than I am with some ideas of resurrection. When visiting my fundamentalist evangelistic relatives as a child, I was introduced to passages in the Book of Revelations that to me were quite nightmarish. Heaven was described as a city foursquare. I never knew foursquare what—feet? blocks? miles?—but whatever, it sounded cramped and restrictive. With streets of gold and "no night there," it seemed a hellish long way from the moist, mossy, dappled place I pictured Heaven to be. As one who loves the cool and dark and can get way too much hot and bright, I wasn't ready to sign up. Outside Heaven's gate (I pictured a cyclone fence like the one surrounding my grade school, and later my imagination added razor-wire to the top), the people who didn't make the "A" team—people I knew and loved—would entwine their fingers in the fencing wire, weeping, wailing, and gnashing their teeth. The thought made me sick. Now, as I see images of desperate people hiding from bullets and searchlights to find a way into the paradise I was fortunate enough to be born in—hoping, groping, dreaming of a better life for themselves and their families—I am back inside that awful childhood nightmare.

Although I am reasonably comfortable with the idea of my own death, loss—the death of someone close—is quite another matter. When my dear friend Hannah died I felt dizzy, nauseated, disoriented. I wolfed two chocolate bars and the remainder of a glass of wine David had left, barely aware of what I was doing. I got hives, then shingles. I felt personally diminished, worth less.

It wasn't until after a conversation with our college-age granddaughter that I began to understand the extent of my response. Joking on the phone, I pretended not to recognize Celina's voice and told her that I could know who *I* was only after *she* had identified herself. If she was my granddaughter, then I was her grandmother. Otherwise, I wasn't. Later, I wondered about the real change of your personhood, depending on your relationships. When my parents died, though I was forty-five, I became an orphan and I felt deeply so. I was no longer someone's child. When Hannah died I missed not only her, I missed part of myself. The part of me that was Hannah's friend died with her. And with the loss, I was ever more determined to make the most of whatever time on Earth I have. But, as can be expected in life, setbacks arise.

"Your ear drum is 90 percent gone," the doctor said. I fought tears, anguished that I might not be able to listen to the songs of birds or the voices of my grandchildren.

For over a year I had had a stubborn ear infection, at first violently painful, leading to a perforated ear drum and powerful antibiotics that at one point had supposedly cured it. But the ear always felt clogged. Several months after the original infection, the feeling that something was lodged inside, along with an intense itch, sent me back to the doctor, who told me I had a disintegrating eardrum.

Eventually I shook myself out of my gloom, realizing how lucky I was to have reasonably good health, at least one good ear, and a lifetime of otherwise well-functioning senses. And with time I stopped feeling disoriented from one-sided hearing. I could still hear better than David could, and he didn't grouse. When our old dog Sadie went deaf, our first clue was that she didn't run to greet us when we came home. This was sad for us, but I don't know that it bothered Sadie, who seemed to adjust to a quiet world. I doubt I could accede to such privation as gracefully.

I exult over the sound of the wind in the trees, the clatter of falling leaves, the haunting evening tremolo of the screech owl. I love being able to differentiate the joyful rising and falling *chirrup cherroo* of the robin from the slightly hoarse robin-like song of the western tanager and the drunken, burbling, robin-like song of the black-headed grosbeak. I mark the approach of spring each year by the night-time concerts of amorous chorus frogs.

I can't imagine not being able to hear a saxophone crooning, a piano's crashing bass and tinkling treble, a violin's sonorous tones. I remember a time when a friend's recorder playing brought me to tears. And the feelings well up inside when I listen to the recorded cries of a newborn granddaughter, or her precious telling when she was not yet two of a trip to a Monet exhibit.

My mother could hear whole symphonies in her head. My auditory memory isn't that good, but even if I can't reproduce the sounds in my mind's ear, I can certainly remember the thrill, the awe, the love engendered by the hearing.

I think more about hearing than I do about taste, but I do enjoy diverse flavors. I nibble on fresh lung-lichen, savoring the Romaine-lettuce texture combined with an essence of mushroom, and I love munching pepper cress and tangy sheep sorrel when I weed the garden. What could be sweeter than a good strawberry warmed by the sun or fresh-picked peas or raspberries? And I'm all but addicted to crisp juicy apples and tough, tangy local dried prunes.

A friend of mine has lost her sense of smell and therefore can taste very little. Perhaps that's how she stays so slim. There are times when having muted olfactory nerves might not be such a bad thing—when the cat box is overdue for replenishing, when something unidentified spoils in the refrigerator, when mice nest in the cupboard. My husband says, "I can't smell it" when I complain about such things. But I would consider it a real loss not to be able to smell forest soil, baskets of fresh basil and cut lavender at the Farmers' Market, a mushroom's musty fragrance, the sweet smell of cottonwood buds in the spring.

Fragrance evokes memories as well. The smell of bread just out of the oven, steaming apple and mincemeat pies, or applesauce simmering on the stove carry me back to my mother's kitchen. Fusty smells of gardening chemicals grab at my heart with memories of my father. Pipe tobacco fresh from the can and the lingering smell of tobacco in wool bring back my fascinating, ornery grandfather. The perfume of warm fir resin, rain on dry earth, a rose from the garden, sun-dried clothes, all take me back to my childhood. I want to pay attention to and remember the tastes and smells and the swelling inside of me that precedes the deep sigh "Aaaah!"

Lupi, our granddog, who lived with us for the eighteen months her family was out of the country, could hear cars coming and ran to heel at our sides long before we were aware of approaching danger. I appreciate being able to hear and smell, but realize I'm nowhere in the league with Lupi. Lupi, however, does not have tremendous vision. Once we found her barking furiously, her hackles high, at the black wheelbarrow parked in the drive near where we had, a few weeks earlier, seen a female black bear.

My mother-in-law has macular degeneration, which I've heard described as being like holding a nickel in front of your eyes. She can no longer read—one of her major pleasures—and she can't recognize faces unless they are quite close. I'm all too aware that eyes age, get clouded over with cataracts, get various diseases. Mine are not nearly what they once were. I remember an ophthalmologist saying I had the eyes of a U-2 pilot, and at one time I could see the spots on the backs of spider mites when the mites themselves were considered visible only under magnification. Now I need glasses to read or do any close work, and I make out distant highway signs much later than I used to.

The psalmist said, "I will lift up mine eyes unto the hills, from whence cometh my help." My help, my inspiration, my therapy come from the hills and meadows, from the plants and animals, from the rocks and rivers. I headed for the hills and walked and walked after September 11. I walk when I feel ill and when my energies are high. I walk to unravel knotty problems or to quiet my mind. I breathe in the natural world; I feel the forest duff or sand or rocks under my feet; I listen to the squirrels and the birds, but most of all, I look.

I love watching clouds. I remember one wonderful moment watching the gathering nimbus, seeing a darker cloud scudding across the face of the gray. I watched, transfixed, as it began to change direction. What kind of wind pattern could cause that? And then, to my astonishment, it shattered to a hundred pieces and the pieces became birds flying in one direction, banking, turning, and continuing in another.

The angle of the sun, the color of the sky, the activity of animals and development of plants tell me the time of day and the season of the year. And as vision informs the hour and the season, so too it informs relationships. Words cannot express what is said by a downcast or misty eye, a trembling lip, white knuckles, a stifled smile. Perhaps without vision I could develop other senses? Hear a change of tone, a quaver, a quickening of the breath?

I hope I can operate as optimistically as my mother-in-law does, or fearlessly like Issa if I'm unlucky enough to lose my sight. But meanwhile I want to absorb the images, suck the marrow from each moment, ask my mind's eye to take lasting photographs and file them in easily retrievable files in the back of my brain so that I can see forever what I have been blessed to have been able to see once.

I wonder how well I could develop my sense of touch if I were more dependent on it. The bark of a cedar tree with its long, fibrous strips should feel very different from the irregular ridges and fissures of a Douglas fir's rough bark or the thick bark of ponderosa pine, which flakes off in thin puzzle pieces. Could I identify them by feel? I know I could tell the prickly needles of a spruce tree from the soft ones of a Douglas fir, and it should be easy to differentiate the scaly needles of cedar from the short, widely spaced needles of hemlock. If I practiced, exercising my sense of touch as if it were a muscle, perhaps I could recognize even without vision many of the plants that are an important part of my life.

When a friend's cancer in her spinal fluid swelled her once strong legs and rendered them totally insensate I was tremendously relieved that she wasn't in pain. But for myself—and the day may come when I think I'm crazy for ever having had such a thought, yet oh, dear lord—I think I'd rather hurt. Pain tells me I'm still alive. That body part is still working. What must it be like to have no sensation, no function?

I most want to appreciate the senses I have moment to moment. I want never to take them for granted or to forget, immersed in a chattering, chaotic mind, to use them. My body operates only in the here and now. I am aware of sensations only with the attention of my brain. I'd like to invite my mind to join my body in the moment. Inside my jumbled mind I walk alone, but when I truly see and hear, smell and feel, I commune with my fellow earthlings, two-legged and otherwise; I am at home in this amazing and intricate system and I am alive.

Chapter Eighteen

Winter gives time to meditate on life and death, dormancy and reawakening, decay and reincarnation. Winter is also a time of promise and potential. Seeds push embryonic roots deep into the ground; tubers, rhizomes, and roots swell, branch, and lengthen; insect eggs wait beneath leaves in the forest duff; animals curl in mud, in hollow trees, under brush piles, inside eggs; buds expand on bare branches; moss capsules swell; owls and frogs call for mates. The world is in gestation.

Newcomers to the Northwest often find winter's lack of light—the sun's low angle, the shortness of the days, the gray skies—depressing. If I had to spend my day inside, I probably would as well. But I was either born with webbed feet and slug slime or acquired them at an early age. If I get itchy for spring, the antidote is a trip outside in boots and raingear. Outside it is obvious that nature is not asleep. She is gathering herself, picking up the tempo, getting ready to burst. The anticipation, like that of a maternity ward, is palpable.

Winter in our hills is the Time of Possibility. Each year as thistles go underground and blackberry leaves turn to mulch, I think, *This year I'm going to get on top of it*, and each year when spring rolls around, I'm still buried.

In the dormant season, numerous nursery chores press for attention. Many seeds need winter's chill to break their dormancy, so this is a critical time for sowing. I begin around October and try to finish before March. If seeds needing a cold treatment don't get enough total hours below a given temperature, germination will be delayed an entire year. Some of these go outside for the winter but others, like oceanspray and dogwood, I put into plastic bags of moist vermiculite and sneak into a bottom drawer in my son's refrigerator. I must sow tiny seeds near the surface because their endosperm doesn't store sufficient energy to push up through deep layers. From fleshy fruits like elderberries, currants, and cascara, I remove the pulp, which may contain germination-inhibiting chemicals, and wash the seeds well. All go into a non-fertile seedling mix with good drainage and moisture-holding capacity. All are covered with hardware cloth or a spun nylon cloth that will, we hope, protect seeds and seedlings from birds, bugs, and rodents.

I get another chance on cuttings in the winter, too. Many root best when stuck in cells of coarse mix in late summer, but there is a second opportunity after the leaves drop, with the next round in winter before leaf-buds break. Depending on the weather, it's also a time to move plants to bigger pots and to pot bare-root plants.

One mid-January day I was attacking the soil pile, digging deep to find loose material well below the two-inch frozen crust, when out rolled a furry golden lump somewhat bigger than a tennis ball, its head tucked into its belly, over-sized hind feet cradling its head, long tail circling in three concentric rings. Worried that I might have hurt it with my vicious stabbing of the pile, I held it in my gloved hand to check for damage but found only a spot of mussed fur. I saw no sign of breathing, nor did I see any sign of fear. It didn't appear to be feigning death. The little creature looked fat and healthy but apparently was in a deep torpor, and I had removed it from its winter burrow. With a lot of potting ahead, I would be decimating the pile, so it couldn't go back there. Finally, I decided to include the little guy in my potting. I put soil and moss in a gallon pot and placed the sleeping fur ball gently on top. I snuggled a moss blanket around it and added another thick layer of soil. Then I tucked the pot under the edge of a tarp and crossed my fingers.

It turned out this was a Pacific jumping mouse, *Zapus trinotatus, Zapus* meaning *big foot*. Its four-inch body can have a tail more than five and a half inches long. Using its long tail for balance, it is able to jump to four feet high, pushing off with its *zapuses*. As it leaps from side to side, it is sometimes mistaken for a frog. The jumping mouse is the lone hibernator among all of our mice and voles, remaining in a deep sleep for more than half the year. One reference said that it lowers its body temperature to two degrees Celsius for the duration, after doubling its body weight in preparation for the long snooze.

I had only recently discovered we even had jumping mice here. One time during the summer I was cleaning up in front of the house and picked up a piece of wood with an unusual furry black fungus (I thought) on it. It wasn't one I'd seen before, so I looked more closely and realized it was breathing and it had two heads. The book says they're born hairless, with eyes still closed and ears folded. So these furry fellows, scrunched tightly side by side, were not brand new, but were certainly very young— less than a month, from what I read. I asked David if he'd seen them. He said, "Oh. You mean that black fungus?"

The Pacific jumping mouse is described as having an olive to nearly black back and orange-ish sides, with the fur getting lighter before hibernation. From my limited observation I would guess their baby fur is darker to make them less conspicuous and, in my little potted friend at least, very little dark fur is apparent during its winter sleep.

The trailer is a better place for sleep than for being awake at this time of year. It has no insulation and walls of thin metal, allowing the temperature inside on a winter morning to drop to the low thirties Fahrenheit, rising only rarely above forty. But a match to the propane jet ignites that familiar PHOOM, the fire roars, and the trailer heats quickly. Unless it's particularly cold and windy it can go from forty to eighty in a half hour. At least part of it can. Even as I'm gasping for air and throwing off layers above the waist, my feet and legs are icy and I reach for a lap robe. David, in thermo-reaction as in most things far more insouciant than I, sits comfortably in his chair, neither too hot nor too cold, and I am grateful he gets up before I do, to start the fire.

We listen to the radio most mornings and again as I fix dinner, plus a while into the evening. We mark the days by the programs: Sunday and Wednesday evenings it's jazz; Monday and Tuesday political or social programs; Thursday philosophy followed by more jazz; and Friday is medieval music. David swears at the idiots quoted on the political shows and cheers for the ones we agree with. He listens intently to the jazz, identifying musicians and often recalling incidents in their careers.

One winter evening the lantern was not working and we were out of candles, so I cooked by the light of a headlamp. David, somewhat inebriated, listened to the radio and hummed in the dark with the monks of the Abbey of Chevetogne, on "Millennium of Music." Circles of light and shadow danced on the ceiling above the stove. The stove is like an upright five-gallon tin can with top and bottom removed, supported on metal straps just above a deep round pan where a tube sends gas to feed the central flame. On four-inch straps above the top of the can is a flat metal hat, like an inverted deep-dish pie pan. Light from the spaces above and below the walls of the stove played around the room and illuminated edges of coats and towels hanging above the stove, reminding me to hang my night-shirt there sufficiently before bedtime that it could billow full of heated air and send me cozily to bed. After dinner David headed for sleep. I sat in the dark soaking my feet, reading with the light of our headlamp, and listening to classical music. I don't want for much.

If I were naming moons, I would call January's the Ice Moon. A night in the twenties and puddles are ice-lidded, some with odd-shaped frozen bubbles below. On the ground, saturated fine-grained clay soils freeze and expand, forming fantastic clay forests and villages for tiny inhabitants—inch-high columns, walls, corridors. Ice needles emerge from the soil or hang from shelves of ice—diminutive stalactites and stalagmites. Clusters of slender ice pillars push up frozen clay rooftops and icy filigrees, forming castles and crags and palisades. The little boy in me wants to stomp them for the satisfying crunch and crumble under my feet; the little girl in me wants to flop down on my belly and envision the tiny residents going about their business within their crystal city. I do both, but only in my imagination.

The pond ice is embossed with patterns of palm or fern fronds. No nearby vegetation created these molds. I can only guess it had to do with breezes as the water froze. Silvery frost trims the edges of leaves like sugar rims on cocktail glasses. Some leaves have a crystal of frost at each surface pore, contrasting with unfrosted burgundy or green veins. Scattered frozen dewdrops adorn twigs like glass pearls; fine-branched shrubs such as snowberry become a mass of silver lace. When the low sun warms in its weak, wintry sort of way, I understand sun worship.

I hated freezing rain after a white-knuckled drive a few years back: no traction on turns, no ability to brake, ice-covered windshield wipers doing nothing but accumulating more ice. But we talked ourselves into exploring an icy day on foot, up the road and into the nearby hills. Ice-coated trees and glossy pavement were beautiful, if somewhat other-worldly. Each hair on Lupi's dark, fluffy tail was tipped with white ice. Women pay handsomely to have their hair frosted, and Lupi had it done for free. I suppose, though, those women would not appreciate having to stay in freezing temperatures or below to maintain the look.

We moved carefully: remaining vertical was the goal. Every bare surface was slick. Slipping and sliding, whooping and giggling, we leapt to tall grass clumps to get some purchase. Eventually we reached the mile-and-a-half mark that is our customary turn-around point. Coming down the hill we grabbed low fir boughs. Hand over hand, aging Tarzan and Jane, if our feet should fly we could swing on the boughs. Some dramatic hiking-boot-on-ice skiing got us laughing about cheap thrills. We get our entertainment—our challenges and triumphs—where we can. After skittering down the hill and with about a quarter mile to go on the road to home, I lost it. But that too was a triumph. Splat down on the road and nary a bone was broken. As the years pass, that's quite an accomplishment for this osteoporotic frame.

Around the end of January or in early February, I begin to notice disturbed soil beneath many fir trees. I've not yet confirmed it, but I believe this is the work of truffle-hunting rodents. Someday I'll try to beat them to the harvest and bring home truffles of my own. These underground fungal fruits, which look a bit like small potatoes, are considered comparable in flavor to costly European species.

Our wild fungi are among the most nutritious food available for rodents, but that is only the beginning of the story. A large share of the spores, along with resident nitrogen-fixing bacteria, pass through the rodent's gut unharmed. The bacteria go to work changing nitrogen from the air to a form usable by trees and other forest flora. The spores reproduce to make more truffles, spreading them widely throughout the woods. The truffle—or mushroom in the case of fungi that fruit above the ground—is the spore-producing part of the fungus. The greater part by far is the miles of underground filamentous structures called hyphae that make up the mycelial network or body of the fungus. In many fungal species, the hyphae connect to the root hairs of a tree or other woodland plant to form mycorrhizae (*myco* from the Greek word for fungus and *rhizae,* meaning roots) that collect water and minerals far more efficiently than would the plant roots alone. At the same time, mycorrhizae protect plants from disease, blocking root-rot and secreting antibiotics that suppress pathogenic bacteria. As the plant grows and photosynthesizes, it sends sugars down to feed the mycorrhizae as well as itself. Thus as the rodent eats and excretes, it becomes integral to the weaving of an intricate web of relationships, greatly increasing the health, fertility, and sustainability of the forests.

Many such complex connections are not yet understood. Author, entrepreneur, and mycologist Paul Stamets says that in a single scoop of healthy soil there are more species of fungi, bacteria, and protozoa than there are of plants and vertebrates in all of North America. He refers to fungi as the grand recyclers of our planet, the interface organism between life and death. They release nutrients, fight pathogens, keep alive plants that are essential to the lives of humans and all animals. Some have antibiotic properties; others are able to digest oil from spills and to detoxify ground poisons. And myriad species and functions are yet to be discovered. Their potential is boundless. Meanwhile in our ignorance, rodents are poisoned and soil is sterilized.

Early February 2002, after our old springer Sadie's September night in the blackberries, she awoke quite agitated. She got herself stuck between the heater and the file cabinet at least a half dozen times. She let herself out twice, which she hadn't done in months. Shortly after lunch she was outside, knocking over and climbing on pots, zooming back and forth. Then she started barking a strange low bark and frothing at the mouth. I panicked, called the nearest vet (in Veneta, thirteen miles north) and took her in. It turned out she was horribly bloated. The vet said this is usually caused by a twisted intestine, but most commonly in big-chested dogs like St. Bernards, and speculated there might be blockage from a tumor. They stuck a needle in her stomach, deflating it just as you might a beach ball, and her tension immediately eased. Then they pumped her stomach and gave her electrolytes because she showed symptoms of being in shock. The vets said she might bloat again but she might get better.

Her color and breathing improved, but when we brought her home she just wanted to sleep. That night around 10:30 she began to complain. Her stomach seemed tight so I massaged it. She burped a few times but seemed jittery for the better part of an hour. I gave her some homeopathics and massaged her some more. She calmed and went back to sleep.

Four days later, Sadie just slept. She didn't get up and she didn't eat. She did quite eagerly drink water from a sponge, but when I added chicken soup to it, she turned away. She was apparently ready to die but had either a strong heart or strong will. I had hoped she would do it by herself, but finally decided she needed help. When we brought her back from the vet, we buried her beside Issa, beneath the dogwood tree. The saddest thing about dogs is the short span of their lives compared to ours. You get deeply attached. They are real members of the family. And then they're gone.

Chapter Nineteen

*Winter—and sometimes even fall—*can bring spine-tingling wind storms. These have most extreme effects when the ground is so rain-soaked that tree roots hold only loosely. In the winter of 1996, our neighbor watched twenty Douglas firs fall across his driveway. It took him and his son-in-law six hours with two chain saws to cut through what had come down in ten minutes. Two years later more than two hundred trees fell on our property, either directly blown or knocked, domino fashion, by trees falling nearby. Fortunately, most dropped where we could leave them for wildlife habitat and eventual decay. A two-trunked oak split both ways; several firs fell across the road and whole swaths of small trees lay on top of each other, roots torn from the soil. Bright shards of wood rose like spears where trees had broken, some near the ground, some snapping high up the trunk. News reported trees splitting cars, houses, barns, and fences; horses, cattle, and sheep running wild. On our hill the power was out for days, but we were oblivious that our neighbors were shivering in their dark, still houses, as we continued as always, with propane to light our lantern, warm our bodies, and cook our food.

Our most memorable wind storm was February 7, 2002, but it wasn't the storm itself that made it memorable. Although we had little damage, the nearby cell tower was down, so we had no way to pick up our voice mail. Service was restored February 10, bringing us news of a granddaughter, born the previous day. Camila Elena Rose Hess-Neustadt was six pounds two ounces, and had dark curly hair. Nearly five-year-old Tasha and her parents were thrilled, and we could hardly wait to meet her. Some day I should ask her if the wind blew her in.

In western Oregon most winter days are mild, gray, and frequently drizzly. Wind storms are momentous as are real downpours. Snow is uncommon enough to be a big deal. When it comes it's usually wet, perfect for making snow forts and families, the great soggy fluffs poured from giant vats in the sky. On a clear night after snow, the moon and Jupiter reflect off sparkling ground and flocked trees, making an evening walk seem almost like day.

I remember a year freezing rain followed a heavy snow, encasing yellow, red, brown, and green stems in ice. Shrubs were weighted down and bent over, like old women with crumbling bones, their long hair trapped under a layer of snow. Sun and warm air moved in and trees cracked, popped, and thwanged as they shed extraneous twigs and branches, along with chunks of ice and clumps of snow. A neighbor pushed snow off the road with the blade of his International Harvester, leaving irregular lumps covered with ice alongside, a parade of blunt-nosed white seals gathered beside the road to cheer on the sliding cars. On the hill where no tracks had broken the snow, the shiny coating of ice, a half-inch or more thick, looked artificial—an endless plastic landscape, or perhaps sugar-syrup icing over the hills, hummocks, and swales. Walking along, we cracked and crunched, hammering our heels through the ice with each step. Suddenly I was running down the hill, crashing through the snow with great bounding strides, exhilarated, giddy, snow flying ahead of landing feet. I felt as if I were flying myself. Wondering how far in the wake I'd left David, I turned to see him leaping, laughing, right behind me. I picked up a handful of snow from beneath the crust—soft, light, barely even cold—a handful of nothing, of frozen air, of crystallized cloud. When I popped it into my mouth, it filled the space and disappeared, scarcely wetting my tongue.

We trekked back up the hill in deep, wet snow one day, past trees with snow-heavy branches pushed close to their trunks. Shrubs became weird creatures hidden beneath thick white blankets or bent low at each side of the path, bowing and scraping. Slogging up hill, snow above boot tops, calves aching, sun shining, we opened our coats and I shed my hat as well. Tree gods, spoiling for a fight, tossed down great pillows of snow, a rain of snow clods, heavy dustings of powder. Having no defensive armor nor an arm strong enough to sail snow missiles back into the tree tops, I put my hat back on.

Excited, panting, we explored country through unbroken snow. When we first moved to our property, we understood that this hill beyond the road's end was public land, and regularly walked and ran favorite paths, climbing to twelve hundred feet or so, depending on the day. One week a no-trespassing sign was abruptly posted, a new road tore through the land, and trucks piled high with logs rumbled down the hill. I continued walking there, wondering if I'd get thrown in jail, but shredded ground, slash, and new roads obscured our old paths. The bulk of the logs, however, had apparently been cut from areas beyond our regular route. Most of the young trees remained.

After a few months I met a truck-load of men entering the property and asked for the name and number of the owner so I could request permission to continue my jaunts. A fellow said, "Oh, he'd just send you to me. I'm the manager."

I gave him my most innocent face and told him I'd been running and walking there for seven years. He said, "Sure. That won't hurt anything. It's the horses we don't want up here." So we continued using the land for our daily hikes.

This day, with a snow carpet concealing everything familiar, we decided to search for our old trail. David spotted the entrance. I greeted the old route, rushing ahead, eager, breathing hard. We broke into the open and were amazed at how overgrown the old path had become in a few short years, and in the snow, harder to find. Off to the right, a cleared area plunged abruptly down. We wondered if the owners had cleared it, and decided that we should explore it someday.

But for the moment we needed to forge ahead. The path narrowed. We fought branches covered in wet snow, and I began to feel uneasy. Soon I had to admit I'd lost the path. We switched leaders back and forth, saying, "It looks easier down there," or "Let's follow this deer trail." We discovered that big as deer are, they can duck much lower than we easily can, and they don't follow a direct route. We searched, trying new directions, investigating new paths, for an hour or so.

"I'm not worried. Are you worried?" we'd reassure each other. I inwardly counted the hours to dark, remembering that temperatures were expected to get into the low twenties. *Plenty of time. Let's pick a direction.* Neither of us wanted to spend hours going in circles and sporadic snow flurries had concealed our tracks, making them impossible to retrace. We looked for a fence we'd glimpsed earlier; if we followed it, we'd at least have an established course. Wet snow down our necks, thorny blackberries entangling our legs, branches snapping our faces, we weren't worried, we claimed. It was an adventure.

I giggled now and then, "Can you imagine our getting ourselves lost up here?" *My* getting us lost. I was the leader when we went astray. In retrospect, that clear area "we should explore someday" must have been the path. But no telling where it was now. We couldn't have been more than two or three miles from home. That should be no problem at all.

I recalled that my grandmother had been within a mile of her house when she froze to death, but I kept that memory to myself. Besides, Grandmother had been in Montana. This was just the foothills of Oregon's Coast Range.

I decided that if it started getting dark we should find a big tree and snuggle together against its trunk. Dark would come around five—it would be a long night. But meanwhile, we kept going. We weren't worried. It was an adventure.

Occasionally we stopped to catch our breath, to try to analyze and think logically, to remember to admire the winter beauty. Finally we found the fence. Snowberry and blackberries were so dense we could rarely walk beside it, but if we could keep it in sight, it could be our guide. Eventually, standing in a small clearing near the fence, we saw farmhouses and tree plantations far below. If we must, we agreed, we could maneuver down the hill, knock on a door, and ask where the hell we were. Neither of us was thrilled with the idea. We wanted to be successful explorers, to find our way back on our own.

But as we continued, nothing looked familiar. I had been on the hill many times, but never where we found ourselves that day. I hadn't even known there was a deep valley beside the ridge where we were wandering. So ultimately we made our way over the fence, down a sometimes precipitously steep slope with drops and holes hidden beneath the snow, through and around huge patches of blackberries, and finally to the valley floor and a snow-covered tractor-trail to a cluster of houses. Startling a couple of boys who were building a snowman ("Where did *you* come from?"), we got directions, hiked several more miles via roads we knew, and arrived home before dark, maybe five hours after we had left. Our low temperature that night was twenty-one degrees. In Flagstaff, where Erika and her family live, it was minus five degrees. My sister Beth's part of Montana was down to minus thirty. We couldn't live as we do in a lot of other places, but I was glad we hadn't spent the night on the hill even in our comparatively mild temperature.

We rationalized that it was because of the snow that we had lost our way. The snow's thick blanket covered plants and trails, making everything look unfamiliar. But in the spring a couple of years later we tried to understand where we had been—and got lost again. These are not particularly wild areas: second growth, underbrush, blackberries, ridges, and valleys, all very much like my own backyard. One definition of wilderness is a "large, confused mass or tangle." The concern for me, I think, is not the tangle without, but the tangle within: the confusion of judgment that can make even a strange town a wilderness, to say nothing of a strange wild area. Maybe that is part of the challenge that keeps me wanting to explore. *Perhaps this time,* I keep hoping, *I will find my way.*

Snow can come anytime from November until March (I remember a neighbor making a snow Easter bunny one year). Often it doesn't come at all. But unless the woods are coated in white, by mid-February, spring's approach can no longer be doubted. Filbert catkins loosen and lengthen, forming golden veils before their dark trunks. Little snow queen, *Synthris reniformis*, blooms on shaded slopes, poking tiny clusters of lavender bells above green or purple-lined, paw-shaped leaves. Osoberry bells begin to unwind, tree and violet-green swallows catch bugs above the rose haze of alder catkins. Tidy and green, the valley is in its golf-course phase, inspiring me to tidy up as well.

It is time to toss unproductive pots, adding yards of potting mix to a meadow still overly clayey from the excavated pond soil spread there two decades earlier. Time also to get rid of fall-germinated weeds and spread corn gluten in pots and paths where we don't want more germination. A serendipitous discovery at Iowa State University, gluten inhibits germination, but breaks down to nourish the soil.

ISU's Dr. Nick Christians was trying to study the effects on grass of *Pythium*, a fungal disease organism, using cornmeal as a growth medium. Although the fungus didn't establish in the meal, Dr. Christians and his colleagues saw that the grass germinated poorly in the treated plots. Eventually they realized that the gluten was stopping root formation, delivering a natural herbicide with no harm to beneficial insects, soil organisms, or waterways. Besides keeping weeds from germinating, its approximately 10 percent nitrogen boosts the growth of established plants. It's a story I enjoy almost as much as I do the product.

Winter twig colors are still glorious. Lit by low-angle sun or sharply contrasting with snow, bittercherry, willow, red-twig dogwood, vine maple, and ninebark stems glow in shades of yellow, amber, burgundy, orange, scarlet, and rust. Alder bark shines ghostly white, interrupted only by dark patches of moss. Until just a few years ago, I thought alder bark was naturally white, as are some birches. But in fact, it is whitewashed by lichen, and only where the air is clean. In a polluted atmosphere, alder bark is dark.

I could name February's the Bright Twig Moon or Green Meadows Moon.

Mid to late February also brings me back to the vegetable garden, where I exult over garlic's green spears thrusting through the ground and push wrinkled pea seeds into loose soil. I never get over the miracle of germination. I nestle into the soil a hard and tiny mass *and Lo! There is life within. And it shall swell and grow and burst forth, rending the very skin that did contain it. And behold! It maketh a new plant. And it is good.*

Chapter Twenty

Growing our own produce gives me great joy and also helps salve my conscience a bit that we drive excessively. I have read that food purchased at the supermarket has traveled an average of fifteen hundred miles, requiring many times the caloric energy it produces to transport it. I can rationalize some of our gas use by our proportionally smaller demands on the planet for our sustenance.

But I still fuss about driving. When we lived in town we enjoyed walking or biking where we needed to go. And I believe in pedestrian-friendly cities and doing away with sprawl. But I'm afraid I believe in it more for the other guy than for myself. I'm too much of a wilding and I love it in our woods. So for now, we'll continue consolidating our errands into as few trips as possible, and hope that the bus route will eventually extend this far.

Until then, we'll keep driving our old cars; we'll buy clothes at Goodwill, and when at all possible, make do rather than buying new. A friend from Ireland planned to stock up here on resale items before he went home. When I expressed surprise that there were fewer such shops abroad, he gently explained that not all people feel such a need to upgrade as Americans do. If it's still good, if it fits, if it works or can be fixed, why not keep it?

Living as David and I do is a wonderful antidote to acquisitiveness. Should we get new furniture? (To put where? We can't walk by one another without doing a little dance.) How about new clothes? (To moulder in damp drawers and feed the mice?) Electronic gadgets? (As I have joked since we saw a bicycle-powered grain mill, David can't pedal fast enough to maintain the current for those wonderful electronic toys.) There's a pay-off too: as we're without abundant worldly possessions, we're far less affected than many by economic ups and downs. And as we don't have to earn money to pay off consumer debts, our time is freer to use as we choose.

I was never crazy about our hovel of a trailer, but I feel everlasting gratitude for having had the opportunity to learn its lessons. Next to raising my children, this time in the woods has been the most rewarding period of my life. Free from societal expectations and entertainment, we can be ourselves. Without a cozy cocoon to escape from the world of commerce and chaos, we are prodded into the real world. We find our joy in working, playing, exploring, and simply being in our natural environment. And being in nature—which will not wait and cannot be rushed—has even taught me to slow down a bit now and then.

My life has been played *prestissimo* from the moment of my birth. I was a ready-to-pop eight-pound infant after a mere eight months *in utero*— although it's my mother who gets the credit for that. Mother said I gave up naps at twelve months. She would read beside my crib, one hand gently on my head. When I seemed sufficiently quiet and relaxed she would slowly raise her hand and, as if glued there, my head would rise along with it. In grade school I ran—late, usually—the two miles to school. If girls had been allowed to do so at that time, I would have run track in junior high and high school. On hikes I impatiently crashed to the front of the line. Had I been a modern-day child, teachers would likely have recommended Ritalin.

Freshman year in high school, when I filed my first income tax return, I listed nine jobs, several of them simultaneous. I was frequently referred to as a jack-of-all-trades (from which I inferred, "master of none"). In college I continued to work various jobs while taking heavy class loads, and was prouder of the holes in my shoes than embarrassed by my sometimes sub-standard grades. In my forties, inspired by my friend Hannah, I took on road-runs, from ten kilometers to marathons. I graduated to a bit of speed on the track at fifteen hundred and three thousand meters, and began to eye the Western States ultra-marathons of fifty miles or more. Unfortunately, my body and mind weren't on the same page. As joints began deteriorating, I had to admit I probably wouldn't achieve my advertised goal of dropping dead at the end of a marathon when I'm ninety-eight. Still I love to test how hard I can work, how intensely I can live. I figure I'm not here for long, I might as well play my best game all the way to the final bell.

Sometimes, however, I take on too many games at once and discover the balls are dropping all around me. Living here in the woods I'm reminded again and again that most of those games are not such a big deal. The world gets along very well without me pushing it. But when I walk slowly enough to see ruffles of golden shelf fungus, sit ten minutes watching darting dragonflies, stop and listen to the bouncing call of a wrentit, that is when I know what life is all about.

I've decided that what tips the balance in matters of pace is the goal. Sometimes hard work and a good run are pure joy. Sometimes I feel pushed and tense, and then I try to reevaluate the reason for the race. Our then-president said, when discussing the Kyoto Protocol, that our American way of life was not negotiable. That way of life—as represented in popular media—condemns most people to working too many hours at jobs they hate in order to buy things they don't need except to prove, at least to themselves, that they are winners. Here in America we are proud to have the freedom to want. What *I* want is to redefine that American way of life.

David and I have discovered what studies have shown: after basic needs are met, more income doesn't increase happiness. I suppose it comes down to what we feel is our purpose on Earth. If it's to scoop up the most goodies, then it's appropriate to continue in the corporate fast lane. If it's the pursuit of happiness, the path would be different.

We have often agreed that this is a journey we would not have been able to take when our children were growing up. Now I'm not so sure. We would of course have had to build a better nest. Loose construction may work for the mourning dove but a tighter weave is optimal for our species. Maybe with children, we would have exchanged the flimsy uninsulated trailer for a snug cabin of lumber milled from our own trees, but still without electricity or plumbing. Why not?

One thing I've learned is that habitat is far more than a nest. Mourning doves occupy their shabby nests only for hatching eggs and raising young nestlings. Then their range widens to open areas where they search for grain, seeds, or fruit, and thence to trees or thickets to ingest safely what earlier they stored in their gizzards. Unless fruit is plentiful, they visit quiet sources of drinking water. Frequently they will travel a dozen miles or more between feeding and resting quarters. They roost, often communally in non-breeding seasons, and may migrate to Mexico or Central America to spend a warm winter. So also, our habitat includes oak and fir woodlands, the pond and its inhabitants; winter wrens and waxwings, snails and glowworms, voles and bears; pure and precious water; sun to warm our bones and put sugar in green growing things; soil to support those plants along with a multitude of insects, microorganisms, and rodents; the tent by the pond for warm-weather living and the community of Lorane for company.

A child growing up in the simplicity we have known for a decade and a half would be in tune with that larger habitat. She would understand that life requires water, whether it is the life of plants, animals, or that child, and quickly would learn that the water supply is not unlimited, and thus must be protected, conserved, and shared. Children here could explore woods, climb trees, kayak the pond, smear pond-mud on their bodies, watch animals playing, hunting, making a life. Here a child could learn the sounds and smells of the seasons, the mysteries of hibernation and migration; learn who eats whom; learn about day and night, life and death. A child living here could look into the vastness of the night sky at millions of glittering specks and swell inside with the immensity and complexity of which that child is a part. Such a child would grow up understanding that seeds come from flowers, plants come from seeds, and our food, like that of all creatures, comes directly or indirectly from plants. She would learn that what we breathe out the plants breathe in and what the plants breathe out, we breathe in. From an early age that child could see that we and all Earth's organisms are intricately connected.

This hypothetical child might of course have missed other connections. My children ran down the street to play with friends, and were busy with sports teams, and classes in music, art, dance, and gymnastics. But we could have imported other kids and gone on nature walks. They all could have drawn flowers and birds and bugs, or written stories and poems about them. And we could have driven a bit farther and still have gone to the sports workouts. Doubtless some things from urban life would have been missed, but the loss, it seems to me, would not have been so great as that of the seven-year-old, living right here in the green Pacific Northwest, who told me he had never before been in the woods, or that of his friend, who said he'd never before seen a deer.

On going to Walden Thoreau said, "I went to the woods because I wanted to live deliberately, to front only the essential facts of life, and see if I could learn what it had to teach, and not, when I came to die, discover that I had not lived."

Our decision was based on far more prosaic considerations. For us the notion to move to the woods germinated from practical reasons— saving money and driving less. It grew rank in loam over-fertilized by excitement, challenge, and possibilities. David and I were goal oriented. We visualized a beautiful and thriving nursery and garden. And we would prove (to whom? ourselves?) that we were capable of living an unadorned life.

Reality blew in, in the form of failures on the land, the emptying of our savings account, and David's hemorrhage, any one of which could have crushed our succulent notion. We moved from the exciting challenge of doing without to accepting our straitened circumstances as a fact, and from there to an aching realization that most of the world lives at least this simply, but many of them with the true deprivations of disease, insufficient food, unclean water, and no hope. We felt more connected than ever before to the have-nots of the world.

As we spent more time in the seclusion of our hills, our focus shifted from the pressures, noise, and pace of society to the ever-changing world of nature. My desire to learn how to garden in concert with nature—how to fashion a project of my own design on the land without harming the ecosystem—opened a wide world to explore. As I learned more it became apparent I would never learn enough. I could try to understand, but needed to respect all the threads of life's web even without understanding.

I slowly and erratically began to accept the creatures that ate my garden, which pointed the way also to respect for the humanity of people I didn't agree with or understand. With friends or my life partner, I found an analogy in looking out at our trees: If I'm landscaping my grounds, an early decision I must make is what kind of tree I want to share my life with. But once that is resolved, I will be happiest if I let it grow according to its nature. If I expect my oak tree to give me oranges, I'm going to be disappointed. If I am upset about the angle of its branches or where it dumps it leaves, the tree won't care, but *my* days will be tense and frustrated. How much more fulfilling it would be to write a poem to its swelling buds, its changing color, its magnificent growth. Which is not to say I would never grouse about some quirk of development or oddness of habit because, let's face it, I have crooked branches too.

As long as it took me to accept the habits of others, it took me much longer to come to terms with my own crooked branches. I needed to accept my own Inner Reptile, to reconcile myself to that selfish part of my brain that doesn't play well with others. Once I accepted that, I could begin to work on one of my most important lessons from this venture (still being learned)—that it's not, as they say, "all about me."

I never considered myself a particularly self-centered person, but perhaps it's a human condition. How would we have survived to evolve had we not been ever wary of possible assaults, of personal attacks? My first revelation that I have an absurd tendency to take things personally was after I vowed not to make war on the critters, and they continued eating my garden. To my embarrassment, I discerned a glimmer of pique. "Poor me. Don't they appreciate that I've attained a higher level of consciousness? Don't they understand that we're all one?" I had to laugh at myself.

Slowly I began to recognize egocentric reactions elsewhere. Early on I had ceded control, aware that I could neither cause nor stop natural events. And I never thought bad weather or bad fortune were my personal punishment, as I hear some do. I knew I wasn't that important in the big scheme of things. But apparently I still thought I *was* that important in the little scheme of things, taking credit—or blame—for causing the mood of others, even if not of the weather.

My rational mind knew that was ridiculous, but the rational mind is not the seat of feelings. It will however, if I listen, let me know how other parts of the brain are behaving. And it reminds me that just as neither the weather nor the voles care about my personal desires, friends and family have their own concerns as well. I needn't feel guilty or angry or hurt at the words or manner of others. They own them. What I own is the way I respond to them. If I can respond out of love, we'll all be better off.

I now believe that it is this self-centeredness that comprises the suffering the Buddhists speak of, that becomes an earthly Hell of our own making. Living without the noise and pace of civilization I could finally understand that it's really *not* about me and also that feeling otherwise now and then doesn't mark me as a failure. I'm not perfect. I'll never be perfect. And that's okay. My reptile will live on even though accepting it does reduce its power. But recognizing its existence forges one more connection to the suffering of all humankind.

Although our impetus in moving to the woods was far less lofty than that professed by Thoreau, in learning to live deliberately David and I have not only learned lessons of the land but have also been allowed to peek through windows into the self. Had we not moved out here, or had we come for only a year or two, I doubt that path would ever have emerged from life's brambles. I doubt as well that we could have discovered the joy of living by doing and attending to our surroundings, as opposed to acquiring, or sitting and being entertained. Just as, lost in the snow, we were blind to the path home when it was right in front of us, it is easy to be so caught up in the scramble of getting and paying that we are blind to the wonders surrounding us on this awe-inspiring planet.

When we were lost that snowy day, we were lucky enough to find the little snowman builders who could give us directions. I wish everyone could find the path home.

Usually I am completely happy in my woodland home, but sometimes when I look at the sun in the trees or admire flowers on the hillsides, I want to cry. I imagine other forests burned, gardens destroyed, temples bombed. Sometimes I am so filled with the multitude of problems people face that I can hardly breathe. I feel impelled to do something about it. Perhaps I will dedicate the rest of my time on this planet to being a radical hippie socialist feminist crone bitch.

Even as I say that, I wonder what it really means, what I really can do. As my time in the woods has allowed me a keener look within myself, I've had to own being at times angry, petty, or insecure. I assume I am not alone. Left to our own devices, what's to keep us from acting on selfish emotions, savaging each other as well as our Earth home? And if people are cold, hungry, or sick, that's where their focus will be. If they see themselves trapped in a powerless role, they'll likely be hostile or apathetic. If their homes, rivers, orchards are destroyed, they'll feel defeated or defensive. What will keep their Inner Reptiles at bay?

Repeatedly throughout my life I've watched while problems abroad were ignored or exacerbated until the cowboys at OK Corral began pacing toward each other, hands twitching over their holsters. *They can't do it yet again*, I think. What kind of creatures are humans to want to annihilate themselves? Are we *Homo sapiens* or *Homo morus*?

I desperately want, before I die, to see western culture heading toward a path that nurtures rather than exploits the world and its inhabitants. One of the adjectives I used to describe my potentially bitchy future is "radical." A radical change is necessary in order to manage the hundred-and-eighty-degree shift toward care of the entire Earth family and the biosphere on which it depends; to sharing rather than merely acquiring; to enjoying what is here rather than yearning for what is not. But radical is necessary also as the root, the basis, the essential foundation of life. I feel a need to revolt, in the meaning of *re* as back, *volt* as turn. We need to relearn old ways of living with, rather than off of, the Earth.

I am achingly aware that human activities are wreaking havoc on Earth's systems, but I'm no longer worried about the fate of the world itself. The microorganisms—the bacteria and fungi—evolve so fast that they can survive most anything, natural or human-made. They would start a cycle going again. I was amazed some years ago to see how lush the growth had become on Mt. St. Helens, little more than a decade after her spectacular eruption. Scientists had guessed it would take the area fifty years to renew, but they hadn't counted on the microorganisms.

Many species however, including our own, change much more slowly. Through eons, we have evolved for the particular conditions here on earth—the proportions of elements in the air, the temperature range in habited places, the body's requirement for water. We alter the biosphere at our own peril. It would seem apparent that if everything is intricately interconnected, to harm any part is to harm ourselves. The question is: have we evolved enough to be able to understand that? I wonder.

I've been told I should accept that violence and greed are basic human nature. I can't argue with that, but submit that empathy and compassion are human nature as well. I find a great source for optimism in the multitude of organizations throughout the world that are working for peace, justice, local economies, and environmental health. Paul Hawken has documented over a million such organizations and believes there may be as many as two million. Even though mainstream media rarely acknowledge them, many connect and communicate through the Internet.

I see them forming a great web like mycorrhizae form with the myriad roots beneath the ground. As with mycorrhizae, these organizations need not be altruistic. It is not for the sake of the trees that the fungal hyphae expand water- and mineral-seeking root surfaces. They receive the plant's photosynthesized sugars, as the bacteria swarming root tips for their exudates break down organic matter, providing nutrients for the plants. They're not networking to be nice. And I don't have to sacrifice, I don't even have to like the other person, for us to cooperate for mutual gain. But I also don't have to out-do her or beat her up. Life is not a teeter-totter. You don't have to be down for me to be up.

With Earth-wide distribution of diverse groups joining together, we should not have to wait for enlightened leaders to show us the way. A bottom-up movement just might be able to inspire and educate concerned citizens and to pressure politicians to work for the good of the Earth and all of its inhabitants. If together we can accept that the goal is to save humanity—clearly a goal of self interest—the action to be taken will be far different than if the goal were the self interest of imperialism, vengeance, or saving face.

What I'm unsure of is whether such a movement could happen fast enough. As the dripping of the polar ice-caps increases tempo, it threatens to out-pace the sifting of sand grains through the hourglass. Perhaps it depends on what kind of game we choose to play as well as how many players join the team. A finite game (as defined by philosopher James P. Carse) such as football, war, or climbing the corporate ladder, has rules and goals, a beginning and an end, winners and losers. An infinite game is like gardening or raising children. The rules are flexible and the goals change. The aim is for health and balance, not winning. The point of the game is to be able to keep playing. How many of us are willing to play an infinite game? It seems to me the human race would want to. I'm sure the microorganisms will.

Meanwhile, I intend to enjoy what's here while I'm here to enjoy it. And I have work to do. I need to find flying squirrels and the truffles they dig for. I need to follow the *kak* of the pileated woodpecker and the *who-hu-hoo* of the great-horned owl to see if I can locate their nests. I need to mulch the garden and harvest the kale and agitate for saving the world. And I must get ready to welcome back turkey vultures and new colonies of Calypsos.

Almost at the stroke of the spring equinox, the lights begin to dim in the winter twig colors. I imagine I can see them reorganizing their juices as softer tones spread across the palette. New leaves emerge in hues of apple green, bronzy green, gray-green, dusty rose. Rufous hummingbirds sip nectar from red-flowering currant flowers. Snow queen, trilliums, and fawn lilies proclaim the return of spring. Tree frogs chirp, chipmunks chase, and mourning doves return to their tattered old nests. Or perhaps this time they'll build new ones.

Maybe I'll name the moon nearest the vernal equinox the Moon of Hope.

Epilogue

In 2005 we finally had to face the fact that the foundation of our house in town, built in 1929, was caving in. The basement had always been damp and usually flooded once or twice a winter. Two of the walls had been cracked for years, but now the cracks had widened and one wall showed a definite buckle. We could not put off dealing with the foundation and figured that, while we were at it, we might as well make the basement a livable space. That would wipe out what we still had of the loan earmarked for our new house, and require a new loan.

When Jeff said he'd like to buy the house, my hesitation was entirely emotional. I had wanted to be able to give the house to both Erika and Jeff when we died. And we had planned to keep renting it out, letting it be our milk cow, with the idea that we could return to it if infirmity made it impossible to live in the country. But we could not pay for a new basement, pay back loans, and build a house of our own.

So in the summer of 2007, Jeff bought the house in Eugene. We became debt-free for perhaps the first time in our married life—a wonderful feeling. And we have a bit left over that we hope will be enough to build a house.

In the fall the building permit for our Lorane hills property was approved. We've had a septic system installed and a new water line laid from the valve at our property's boundary to the new house site. We're currently working on the excavation, which wants to crumble away in the rain.

We hope to do most of the house construction ourselves. I don't even know how to build things, but I can learn. And I really want the experience and the feeling of being a part of the building of my home. But there's a broken step in front of the trailer that we have been ignoring for six months. Does this comment on our innate fitness as Mr. and Ms. House-Builder? We're currently (in December 2007) seventy-two years old. Are we kidding ourselves?

We intend to hold tight to our frugal habits and to do more and better, eliminating batteries and at least some of the propane, using rain water for many of our domestic needs as well as in the garden, constructing a series of ponds to clean and recycle gray water. Never ever do we want to take Earth's offerings for granted.

Will we meet our goals? Will we get it done before we're eighty? If dreams come true, we surely will. But that's another story.